WRONGLY
CHARGED

WRONGLY
CHARGED
A LOOK AT THE LEGAL SYSTEM

DAVID MERKATZ

Prominent Books

ISBN 10: 1942389035

ISBN 13: 978-1-942389-03-3

Prominent Books and the sunburst compass logo are
Trademarks of Prominent Books, LLC

ACKNOWLEDGEMENTS

I would like to take the time to thank the law firms who worked diligently with the Palm Beach County State Attorney's office to help get these cases resolved.

The Law Offices of Eliot J. Lupkin, P.A., of Fort Lauderdale helped me get through many sleepless nights. Eliot was not only an attorney but a friend to me. As one can imagine, I was very nervous throughout this ordeal, but he was always there to assure me that everything would be fine.

Also, a very special thanks to Tyler Harding, Esq. of the Law Firm of Hoffman & Harding in Boca Raton. I have also known Tyler for many years, and he assisted Eliot Lupkin in dealing with the State Attorney's Office in Palm Beach County. Tyler was very effective in working with the prosecutor and helped all those concerned gain a clear understanding of what really went on in this matter. He worked tirelessly on my behalf, and I will always be appreciative.

I would also like to thank the Law Office of Jeffrey S. Weiner, who helped Josh in this case. He is one of the best criminal attorneys in Florida.

Last but not least, I would also like to thank Mark Durkee of A Signature Bail Bonds. Mark provided a great service in securing a fast bond and my quick release from custody.

I have listed their information here, so anyone reading this book can contact them for assistance:

Law Offices of Eliot Lupkin, PA
1 East Broward Blvd Sutie 700
Ft. Lauderdale, Florida 33306
(954) 767-9200
http://www.eliotlupkin.com

Law Offices of Hoffman & Harding
9070 Kimberly Blvd #57
Boca Raton, Florida 33434
(561) 482-2000
hardlaw@aol.com
http://www.hoffmanandhardinglaw.com

Jeffrey S. Weiner
9130 S. Dadeland Blvd
Miami, Florida 33156
(305) 670-9919
lawfirm@jeffweiner.com
http://www.jeffweiner.com

Mark Durkee
A Signature Bail Bonds
525 S Andrews Avenue
Fort Lauderdale, Florida 33301
(954) 630-0000

Disclaimer

Please note that the author is not an attorney and that this book should not be construed as offering legal advice. It should be noted that unless otherwise stated, all legal references concern federal and Florida state law. If you feel your constitutional or legal rights are being violated, you should contact an attorney in your state.

TABLE OF CONTENTS

PREFACE

It seems that every time we turn on the television, there's a legal show airing. We're fascinated with them; perhaps because whether we watch *The Good Wife*, reruns of *Matlock*, or one of the many reality crime shows, it feels as though we are gaining valuable information about our legal system. Unfortunately, most Americans do not truly understand their rights or how these rights are often threatened by the very people who are supposed to protect them.

I, on the other hand, have witnessed the workings of our judicial system up close and personal. My knowledge was gained not by watching *Law & Order*, but after being unjustly accused of some rather serious crimes. It was through this experience I came to realize that, despite what we're led to believe, we are often treated as though guilty until proven innocent; not the other way around; the way our fair and just legal system was intended.

Throughout this book, I will take you through the facts of my case: namely, that I was trying to run my locksmith business in an increasingly competitive climate; that I had in mind a particular business strategy and that I consulted three separate attorneys to determine whether what I was proposing was legal, and I was assured by all three that, at most, it would be considered trademark infringement—a civil matter. Despite these assurances, however, I would be charged under Florida's money laundering and conspiracy to defraud statutes—felonies that carry serious jail time.

This book was inspired not only by my experiences but also by those who have suffered financial ruin—not to mention mental anguish and the loss of their freedom—after being wrongfully charged. It is my sincere desire to help the average citizen navigate the legal system with issues, including:

The arrest process

- Navigating the bail system (including how to get out of jail before First Appearance)
- The trial process
- Plea agreements (and why so many innocent people accept them)
- Florida's sentencing guidelines
- Appealing a conviction or civil judgment
-

It is my sincerest wish that this book will help others who are wrongfully charged to be able to assert their rights and, hopefully, protect themselves from serious financial distress or ruin, avoiding the necessity to have to rebuild their lives like I am trying to do now.

Please note that I am not an attorney and that this book

should not be construed as offering legal advice. It should be noted that unless otherwise stated, all legal references concern federal and Florida state law. If you feel your constitutional or legal rights are being violated, you should contact an attorney in your state.

CHAPTER 1
My Story

My thirty-five-year career as a locksmith began in Bensonhurst, Brooklyn—the same neighborhood where I grew up. Like many New York City neighborhoods, Bensonhurst in the 1960s was full of middle-class, close-knit families that lived by a code of determination and hard work. People were not necessarily educated in a traditional sense; instead, they lived by their wits and street smarts. The result was an entrepreneurial spirit that could be seen in every mom-and-pop business, from the local laundromat to my own mother's bakery. The prevailing attitude was that with a lot of hard work and a little luck, there wasn't anything you couldn't achieve. You just had to pick something, give it your all, and never, ever give up.

This work ethic was ingrained in me from early childhood, and by the time I was seventeen, I had found my "something". I got a job with a locksmith supplier and began learning the trade. I quickly realized that being a locksmith could be a very lucrative business, and sustainable, regardless of the economy. After all, who didn't need to change their locks at one time or another? People needed new locks after buying a new home or business, or after being burglarized. People locked themselves out of their cars and apartments—often at odd hours—and they needed someone to let them in.

The next step was to get my license, which was required by New York City for all locksmiths. The license could be obtained in one of two ways: either by passing an extremely difficult test or getting two licensed locksmiths to sign a letter of qualification. Well, it wasn't so easy to find locksmiths to do this, since they would, in effect, be helping their own competition. Luckily for me, I had already become friends with several local locksmiths who had come into our shop to purchase supplies. Two of them were kind enough to sign the letter for me.

Obtaining the license was only one part of the process, however. I still had to learn the trade, and the best way to do this was through an apprenticeship. My boss took me on all of his jobs, teaching me how to change the different kinds of locks and how to deal with customers. There was no pay, but I didn't care. I was gaining valuable experience, plus he bought my lunch and even threw me a twenty every now and then. Twenty bucks was a lot of money at that time, especially for a teenager, and I can still remember how it felt when he placed the bill in my hand. It was like I had won the jackpot!

After a year or so, I was ready to put my new skills to the test, and start collecting a paycheck. At age nineteen, I opened my first locksmith shop in downtown Brooklyn. Getting customers was a piece of cake—all I had to do was place a large display ad in the Yellow Pages, and the phone started ringing off the hook. People called me day and night with everything from lock-outs to changing locks to lost car keys.

Everything was going great, but by age 22, I was ready for a change of scenery. I was young, single and had never lived anywhere but Brooklyn. My father, who had moved to South Florida after my parents' separation, asked me to come down there and live with him. Since the one thing I didn't like about New York was the ice and snow, I took him up on it.

When I headed south, I fully expected to have to jump through the bureaucratic hoops in order to get a new locksmith license; so I was shocked to learn that, unlike New York, the state of Florida did not require licensure; in fact, there were no industry regulations whatsoever. All I would need to open a shop was a county tax receipt.

I went down to the office with my ID, only to find that even that wasn't necessary. A very nice lady handed me a form and told me to fill in the name and address of my business along with some incidental personal information. That, in addition to a sixty-dollar fee, authorized me to run a locksmith business. They didn't even perform a criminal background check.

I walked out of there in complete shock. I could not believe the state would allow anyone with sixty bucks to have unfettered access to people's homes and businesses. I didn't dwell too much on it, though; I knew I would run a reputable business, so I knew it didn't have much to do with me.

As I had done in New York, I placed my ads in the local phone book. The bigger the ad, the busier you became, so I bought the largest ad I could afford and waited for the phone to ring. I didn't have to wait long; in fact, for the next three years, I had more business than I could handle and even hired three guys to work for me.

That all changed with the arrival of Home Depot and the other do-it-yourself megastores. They were able to sell the locks to the consumer at distributor cost—which is the same price locksmiths paid for them. Now, when I quoted someone one hundred dollars to install a deadbolt, they'd say, "Why so much? I could buy a lock at Home Depot for ten bucks!"

This was a major problem for everyone in the business, and it was compounded by the fact that no license was needed. Anyone with a screwdriver could call themselves a locksmith, buy a single ten-dollar lock, and undercut our prices. There was no commitment of having to stock up on inventory or anything else. Plumbers and electricians did not face this problem, as they were required by Florida law to have a license to buy certain products and a permit to install them. I had no idea why my trade was different, all I knew was that my business had dropped by fifty percent since Home Depot came to town.

The situation was frustrating, but I hadn't gotten this far without learning how to roll with the punches. I did what most locksmiths were doing: I closed my shop and went mobile. That helped for a year or so, but then a new problem arose. During the first few years of the Internet age, most people still depended on the Yellow Pages to find whatever they needed, whether it was a locksmith, a plumber or a dentist. By the year 2000, however, more than seventy-five percent of advertising was being done online. At this point, in order to keep the phones ringing, locksmiths and every other businessperson had to advertise online in addition to the phone book. We also had to pay for the creation and maintenance of websites as well as the means to drive traffic to those websites.

One of the most efficient ways to do this was—and still is—through pay-per-click ads. The business owner places their ad on search engines such as Google or Bing and then pays every time a potential consumer clicks on that ad, which brings them to their website. Initially, it was a dollar per click to place such an ad under locksmith headings, but over time, the cost literally skyrocketed. Today, I'd have to pay $40-$50 per click to be in the top three listings. This kind of advertising was an enormous financial burden, especially compared to the days of Yellow Pages. Whereas a business pays a flat fee to be featured in the phone book for a certain period of time, Internet ads are subject to change depending on the number of clicks and the number of competitors bidding on "per-click" rates for better placements of their ads. There is no guarantee that people who click on your ad will become customers; even worse, there are many businesses and individuals committing "click fraud"—clicking on ads for the sole purpose of diving up costs for the advertiser. This further ate away at my profits, and I found myself working harder and harder and earning less and less.

By 2006, advertising had become cost prohibitive; it was just too expensive to make the phone ring. Added to this was an influx of immigrants, mostly from the Middle East, who had discovered they could move to Florida, open a mobile locksmith business, and place ads on the Internet. They would advertise cheap online prices, only to "upsell" the job once they were at the customer's home or business. Traditional locksmiths like me could no longer compete.

Again, I had to take a step back, reassess, and figure out my next move. Under the circumstances, the best thing I could come up with was, "If you can't beat 'em, join 'em." So I did away with my salaried employees and my vehicles; then I hired those immigrants, made them use their own vans and tools, and split the proceeds with them.

Despite my efforts, by 2008, the Internet was so inundated with locksmiths that I was struggling to turn a decent profit. My employees would collect 50%, and I was using 35% of my profits just for advertising.

Now truly at a loss, I finally called a meeting with my subcontractors and told them I could not continue to keep the business afloat. I expected them to be upset or even angry about my decision, but instead they told me that they had an idea. It was very simple, they said, and it just may be the solution to my problem.

There were still some large traditional locksmith companies in the area. We would register fictitious names that were similar to those companies', then advertise on the Internet using those names.

That's genius! I first thought when they suggested this, but I soon became concerned. *Is it legal?*

I had lived in Florida long enough to know that their laws are often counterintuitive (at least to a New Yorker). So before committing to this plan, I consulted with three attorneys. The general consensus was, "Well, it's not nice, but it's definitely not illegal."

They advised me that I should be prepared for a civil lawsuit for trademark infringement, but that would be the worst-case scenario. They went on to explain Florida's "fictitious name" statute, which read as follows:

Fictitious Name Statute FS. 365.09

EFFECT OF REGISTRATION—Notwithstanding the provisions of any other law, registration under this section is for public notice only, and gives rise to no presumption of the registrant's rights to own or use the name registered, nor does it affect trademark, service mark, trade name, or corporate name rights previously acquired by others in the same or a similar name. Registration under this section does not reserve a fictitious name against future use.

After speaking to the lawyers and reading the statute, I felt more comfortable moving in this direction. I also noted that the companies whose names we were imitating had also registered under fictitious names; they had not, however, trademarked or incorporated under their legal names. The law clearly stated that using a fictitious name did not "reserve a fictitious name against future use." This struck me as rather absurd, but if it was going to help me save my business, who was I to question it?

As I thought about it further, I realized what a common business practice this was, even by mega corporations like Apple and Samsung. Every day someone comes out with a product that is a variation of something already on the market, and hardly a day goes by that the media doesn't report on how some company is suing another for infringement. However, barring some other complication, it is always a civil matter, not a criminal one.

For example, in 2013, a "big box company" was sued by Tiffany's for selling counterfeit Tiffany engagement rings and putting them in real Tiffany boxes. The company was never criminally charged, though, and I was assured that the same would be true in my case.

Armed with this knowledge, I registered and/or trade-marked five or six names similar to the larger locksmith companies in the area. I also placed Internet ads for lock-smith services using these names and created websites for them. At the bottom of each website was a disclaimer stating that we were not the larger company; it even included a link to that company's site, should the consumer prefer to deal with them. Sure, it was fine print at the bottom of the page, but isn't this true of all disclaimers?

Once that was taken care of, I went back to running my business as I always had: offering every customer a warranty and doing every job perfectly. I never sold counterfeit locks and always treated my customers fairly. When I did receive the occasional complaint, I issued a refund, no questions asked. That's why I had such a good rating with the Better Business Bureau.

That didn't mean I had a good rating with the other locksmiths, however. As expected, the companies that lost business to us were very angry. One filed a lawsuit for using a name similar to theirs, but nothing came of it. Others, however, would tell the customers to complain to the police. Sometimes, the police called me to discuss it. I would explain the situation and ask if I had committed a crime. Since the answer was always no, I would then ask the officer if he or she happened to be friends with the other locksmith(s). Again, their answer was always "no" and that it was a civil matter between me and the other locksmith.

To this I would reply, "So why are you calling me?" They never really had an answer for that one.

So, other than a few ruffled feathers, life—and business—went on, and quite successfully. That is, until late 2013 when I was hiring three locksmiths who showed up for a job, only to discover that it was a "sting" set up by law enforcement. In Chapter 2, you'll read about how my business strategy, while "not very nice" but clearly very legal, resulted in arrests and felony charges.

CHAPTER 2
The Sting

Florida is known for its beautiful beaches and year-round sunshine. But on Tuesday, February 5, 2013, what had started out as a typical bright, sunny morning would turn into a stormy nightmare for one young locksmith. Setting out for what appeared to be a run-of-the-mill job, he had no idea that he was about to walk into a sting operation set up by the police officers of Palm Beach County.

As I mentioned in the last chapter, by 2013, my role in the locksmith business consisted of answering the phones and booking jobs. I would then send out independent contractors to the client's residence or business.

At around 10:45 that morning, I received a call from a woman who said she needed the locks re-keyed at her Palm Beach residence. Re-keying is not the same as changing the locks. Instead, the locksmith removes the lock and changes the cylinder inside so that the old key no longer works; then the original lock is reinstalled and the client is given a new key.

As she was explaining to me where she lived, I could feel my antenna going up. There were noises in the background that I could only describe as suspicious, but I quickly dismissed the thought. I had never second-guessed clients before, so why start now? Besides, it was a simple job, and one we were commonly called to do. I quoted the woman a price of $85, to which she replied, "Okay, come in and do it."

As soon as I hung up with her, I called Josh, one of the independent contractors I worked with. I told him what the client needed and gave him the address; then, confident the job would be taken care of, I went about my day.

When Josh arrived at the house, the woman was pleasant enough. She asked him if he was with ABC Locksmith, to which he replied that he was. It should be noted that as an independent contractor, Josh did work for several area companies; therefore, he would have given her the same answer no matter what company she asked him about. Besides, it was my experience that most customers don't care about the name as long as the job is done right and for a fair price.

Josh quickly set about removing the old lock. He then asked her for the key. When re-keying a lock, the old key is used to configure the inside. She told him she had lost the key, which was presumably why she had called us in the first place. Josh then informed her that there would be an additional charge of $30, since without the key the job would involve more time and labor.

"Okay, go ahead and do it," she replied.

Josh took the lock back to his truck, reset it to the new key, then returned to the house to reinstall it.

When he was done, he tested the lock to make sure it worked. Satisfied with his work, the woman asked if she could make the check out to ABC Locksmith.

"No," he explained, "I am an independent contractor, so please pay me directly."

When she heard this, she fished $115 in cash out of her purse and handed it to him.

Josh had pocketed the money and was about to leave when suddenly the front door came crashing open. He stood there, frozen, as Palm Beach police officers entered the house and surrounded him.

"Sir," the one of them said as he slapped handcuffs on him, "you are under arrest for grand theft, obtaining property by false personation and burglary of an occupied residence."

Right now you may be asking why the Palm Police Department got involved in this at all. As it turned out, they had been receiving complaints from ABC Locksmith, which was one of the larger locksmith companies in the area. They also happened to be one of the companies whose names I had emulated and registered, and they were angry that I was getting some of their business. Most importantly, they did all the locksmith work for the Town of Palm Beach, including the police department. So, instead of advising them that this was a civil matter and they should file a lawsuit against me, the cops decided to help them.

After cuffing Josh, they read him his rights, including his

right to remain silent. Completely confused as to what was happening, Josh didn't say a word as he was led out to the police car like a common criminal.

Once at the police station, however, he endured hours of interrogation about his business practices before being taken to the Palm Beach County Jail for booking.

I'm sure, like most people, that Josh was waiting for the cops to tell him he could make his one phone call. After all, this is how it works on all the TV shows, right? On every crime show from *CSI* to *Law & Order*, the "perp", regardless of what he is arrested for, is allowed to call his mother, his attorney, or anyone else he thinks can help get him out of jail.

Unfortunately, this is not true in real life. The reality is that it is very rare to be allowed a phone call after arrest. Instead, you are either being grilled by cops or sitting in a jail cell, sometimes for hours, while your family and friends wonder and worry where the heck you are.

Even if someone thought to come looking for you at the local jail, the cops wouldn't be able to tell them anything. That's because, until you are booked, you're not in the system. You're in some kind of no man's land. You know you have rights, but you're finding it impossible to exercise them. This is true whether you have been arrested for murder or for a traffic stop.

After being interrogated, Josh was placed in a cell for several more hours before being formally charged. At that point, he would also learn the amount of bail for each charge.

I can only imagine how he felt when the clerk read off the charges and bond amounts: "$5,000 for the grand theft charge, $3,000 for the false impersonation. NB on the burglary charge."

"Excuse me? What's NB?"

"That means no bond, sir."

In Florida, burglary is considered a life felony crime; therefore, bail can be set only in front of a judge, and at his or her discretion.

Since Josh had already spent the entire day in jail waiting to be charged, he would have to spend the night in jail. He was, however, finally able to make his phone call and at least let people know where he was.

Fortunately, the next morning, the judge noted that Josh had no prior arrests and assigned a bond amount of $5,000 on the burglary charge. A total of $13,000 for showing up to re-key a lock! After posting his bond, Josh was taken back to his cell for another eight hours before finally being released. You can see the documents regarding Josh's arrest at the end of this book.

Josh was out of jail, but the Palm Beach PD was not finished with us yet—not by a long shot.

On February 7, 2013, Peter, another independent contractor, received an interesting phone call.

"Hey, how ya doing?" the man said when Peter answered his phone. By his tone, Peter would have thought they were old friends, except for the fact that Peter had no idea who he was. The man then introduced himself as "Officer Nick," the same cop who had arrested Josh.

"Peter, we're conducting an investigation into some unsavory business practices, and I would really appreciate it if you could come down to the station for an interview."

Peter, who knew all about Josh's ordeal, replied, "Am I going to be arrested?"

"Arrested? Of course not! Peter, I'm just asking you to come in, answer a few questions. It would really help us out."

Peter told Officer Nick that he would think about it, then he called me. I immediately told him not to go.

"Why not? He told me I wasn't going to be arrested."

"And you believed him?"

Like many people, Peter thought it would be easier to comply with a request from the police. He also believed the officer when he said it would just be an interview. But what most people are not aware of is that in the course of an investigation, it is perfectly legal for a police officer to lie to a suspect, person of interest, or just about anyone else. They can say whatever they have to in order to get you there, and once you are, they can interrogate and even place you under arrest.

I then reminded Peter that under the law, he was not required to go at all. "Let him get a warrant for your arrest," I told him, "or ask him to conduct the interview by phone."

I guess I wasn't persuasive enough, though, because on February 8, Peter called the detective back and scheduled the interview. It was the worst mistake of his life. After being subjected to hours of grueling interrogation, he was arrested and charged with burglary of an occupied residence and grand theft.

Like Josh, Peter was then transported to the Palm Beach County jail and booked. Hours later, the charges and bond amounts were read to him: $3000 for the grand theft and no bond on the burglary. Since it was too late to go before the judge, he had to spend the night in jail as well. The next morning, the judge gave him a $3000 bond on the burglary charge. I have included the documents regarding Peter's arrest at the end of the book.

Peter posted bail as soon as he could, but he still had to wait another six hours until he was released. This is another thing most people don't know: the cops are in no rush to release you, even after bond has been posted.

Like everything else in the penal system, it's all about procedures; and if you have the misfortune of being arrested, you will be subjected to several such procedures—some more unpleasant than others—before your release can be secured. This is true, no matter what crime you are accused of.

When you are arrested, the first thing the cops do is search you for drugs, weapons, or anything else incriminating. Then you are put in a cell for approximately two to four hours. You may be examined by the jail doctor who can draw blood to check for drugs and even swab the inside of your mouth to get a saliva sample. This enables them to run your DNA to see if it has been linked to other crimes, or—just as frightening—keep it on file. Then, you are returned to the cell to wait for another three or four hours until the formal charges are read to you.

At this time, you are allowed to make a phone call and hopefully get a hold of someone who is willing and able to help you post bond. During this, the cops run a complete warrant check to make sure you don't have any other outstanding warrants. Then, if you're all clear, you will be processed out, which takes yet another six to eight hours. So, essentially, we are talking a total of sixteen to twenty-four hours from time of arrest to release; that's if you're given bail and if you can post quickly—two big "ifs".

After what happened to Josh and Peter, I knew they were coming after me next. Well, they weren't going to catch me by surprise. I retained an attorney so that when the time came, I would be prepared.

Given the zeal with which they had gone after two independent contractors, I was sure my own arrest was imminent; however, months went by without a word. Well, no news might be good news, but in this case, it was also extremely nerve-racking. Every day, I tried to go about my business, but I was always waiting for the axe to fall.

By April of 2013, I couldn't stand the suspense anymore. I called my attorney and asked him to please find out what was going on. When he called the detective, the officer tried to pull the same thing as he had with Peter;

he asked if I would come down to the Palm Beach police station for questioning. Well, there was no way that was happening. I told my lawyer that the detective could come to Broward County, where I lived. Of course Officer Nick refused because, as I well knew, they could not arrest me in Broward without a warrant; that's why he was trying to lure me to Palm Beach. He called my lawyer several times, trying to get me there, but I knew it would be a one-way trip.

"Let him get a warrant," I had said.

There was radio silence after that, and several more months went by with no word. Again, I was happy that I hadn't been arrested, but that did not mean I was happy-go-lucky. I spent many sleepless nights wondering whether the cops would ring my bell, wake up my family and drag me out in cuffs. I didn't know how much longer I could take this.

Then, on Friday, August 16, 2013, I got the call I had been dreading. "Bad news, David," my attorney said as soon as I answered the phone, "they have a warrant for your arrest."

The first thing I wanted to know was what they were charging me with, but the lawyer couldn't tell me, as the warrant was sealed. This scared me to death. They had charged Peter and Josh with very serious crimes, and they were only independent contractors. What would they do to me, the supposed "mastermind of the scheme"?

As upset as I was, I had to admit that it had been very courteous of the detective to call my attorney. By law, he could have simply handed the warrant to the Broward sheriff, who would have then surprised me with an arrest.

Officer Nick did request that I surrender to Palm Beach the following Monday.

"Do me a favor," I told the attorney. "Delay him until Wednesday so I have time to research the charges."

The detective was only too happy to give me the extra time; after all, he thought he was making the arrest of his career! I knew that if I went to Palm Beach, he would keep me, the "big fish", there for the media; then transport me to the jail. Little did he know that I had no intention of surrendering on his turf.

He also didn't know that I had sources who could provide me with valuable information ahead of my arrest. Specifically, I was hoping that one of these sources would be able to unseal the arrest warrant and see what they were charging me with.

I reached out to a friend that Friday, and by Monday, he had an answer for me. I thought I had been prepared for anything, but when I heard the words "organized scheme to defraud (a felony), obtaining property by false impersonation, and money laundering," I thought I was going to throw up. Remember, this was all because I had registered names that were similar to other locksmith companies—a practice that three different attorneys had advised me was not a crime!

My source also had some good news for me. I would be given bond on all of these charges, for a grand total of

$19,500 (I have included them at the back of the book). He also reassured me that there was no Nebbia attached. (The topic of Nebbia will be discussed in the chapter on bail bonds. For now, suffice it to say that this was a great relief.)

Now that I knew the amount of the bond, I reached out to my good friend and bail bondsman, Mark Durkee. After telling him my story, he agreed to meet me the following morning to fill out the bond paperwork. Once I did this, I would have everything in place for a quick release. I was feeling better already.

Now all Mark could do was wait. Bondsmen cannot post bond until the charges are formally read; however, they do have access to the jail's computer, so they can literally post seconds after the accused's name is in the system. I wouldn't even have to use my one phone call!

On Wednesday, April 21, 2013, my friend took me to surrender myself, but not to Officer Nick. Instead, I went to the main jail. It was within my rights to do so as long as the warrant was satisfied, but I knew he would be none too pleased by my decision.

At around 9:30 a.m., I walked in and told the clerk I was there to turn myself in. Her head jerked back in surprise, and her eyes flicked around the lobby as if to make sure this wasn't some reality show prank. "You're joking, right?"

"No, I'm afraid not."

When she realized I was serious (and possibly crazy), she

did a search for the arrest warrant. When she found it, she told me to wait and that a cop would come for me.

At 9:45, an officer did come out. He was looking at me much like the clerk had.

"What are you doing here?" he asked as he snapped the cuffs on me. He looked even more confused after I'd given him a brief summary of my story. "I would think that's a civil matter."

"It should be, but we pissed somebody off."

Shaking his head, the cop took the handcuffs right off. "Let me see what I can do to help you."

I told him that I already knew the charges and had a bondsman. I guess most people are not so well-prepared, because he had that surprised look again. "Okay, that will make it go much faster," he said, trying to be reassuring. "I'll get you out of here as fast as possible."

They were treating me very well, but even I was shocked when they called me at 10:11 to have the charges read. Less than a half-hour? It had to be a record! Then Mark Durkee could do his thing and post my bond. Of course, I still had to go back to the cell so they could run the warrant search.

At 2:30 that afternoon, my name was called, and I was taken downstairs to be processed out. By 2:55, I was out the door. It had been only five hours since my arrest—far less than the normal eight to ten hours most people deal with. In fact, I was probably out before the Palm Beach detective even knew what was happening. I knew he had to be ticked off that I had gone around the system and robbed him of his moment of glory.

But, as I explain in the following chapters, my ordeal was still far from over. These chapters will cover bonds, first appearances, and how to get out of jail before seeing a judge.

Chapter 3
Keep Your Friends Close and Your Bail Bondsman Closer

Navigating the Bond System

When I tell people that everyone should carry around the name and number of a local bail bondsman, they look at me like I'm nuts. That's because most people believe that if we follow the laws and are good little boys and girls, we will never get into trouble—that even if we happen to be arrested, the authorities will immediately realize their egregious mistake and let us go. In this chapter, I will illustrate that this is simply not the case and explain the workings of the bail bond system.

Take, for example, a friend of mine, who we'll call John Smith. One day, John was pulled over for a routine traffic stop. When the cop asked for his license and registration, John handed it over without a thought, because that's what a law-abiding citizen does. An officer makes a request, and you comply. John figured the cop would run the license, then issue either a warning or ticket, so you can imagine his surprise when the officer returned, hand on his gun, and ordered him to step out of the car. The conversation went something like this:

"Mr. Smith, you're going to have to come with me."

"Come with you … for a traffic stop?"

"Mr. Smith, there is an open warrant for your arrest."

"What?"

The next thing John knew, he was handcuffed, placed in the back of the police cruiser, and taken to jail. He had no idea what was going on, but his mind was racing with all sorts of horrible things. *Will I have to stand trial? What if I'm convicted of some horrible crime? What if I can't afford a good attorney?* And the biggest one of all: *How is this even happening to me?* Even though he knew he hadn't committed a crime, he was completely at the mercy of the system, and the uncertainty was terrifying.

It took several hours before the cops discovered that there was another John Smith with a similar date of birth; he was the one wanted, and on a felony charge. My friend, John the law-abiding citizen, was released, but he'll never forget feeling so utterly powerless.

Another friend of mine, J.J., went through a similar experience. While he's an honest and all-around good guy, J.J. can be a little heavy on the gas pedal. One day, while driving along the interstate, J.J. was pulled over and ticketed for speeding. In addition to the fine, he was ordered to take a four-hour defensive driving class. J.J. wasted no time in signing up for traffic school, and at the end of the class, he received his certificate of completion—another copy would be sent to the Department of Motor Vehicles.

Satisfied that he had done his due diligence, J.J. went about his business. The problem was that, unbeknownst to him, the DMV clerk never entered the certificate of completion into the system; therefore, as far as the DMV was concerned, J.J. had not complied with the terms of the court order.

Six months later, he was pulled over for a routine traffic stop. Like John Smith, J.J. wasn't worried when he handed his license and registration to the cop. And like John, he was flabbergasted when the officer informed him that he had been caught driving with a suspended license.

It's important to note that the system doesn't let the police officer know why a license has been suspended, only that it was. And since driving with a suspended license is a criminal misdemeanor charge, they handcuffed J.J. and placed him under arrest. His car was impounded, and he was taken to jail.

Now, remember, this was a guy who never did anything wrong in his life, but he was about to get a taste of how the other half—the criminal—lives. It would be sixteen hours until he was booked and given a bond amount of $100, and since he didn't have any idea as to how the system worked, it took him an additional twelve hours to figure out how to bond out.

A few weeks later, he brought the certificate to the DMV and had his license reinstated. Of course he received no apology whatsoever for their mistake, as it is the responsibility of the individual to check that the certificate of completion was entered into the system.

So, here is an honest guy with a clean record who spent almost two days in jail, paid $100 to get out of jail and another $200 to get his car out of the impound lot, all because of a clerical error. Three months later, the state dropped the charges, and he did get his bond money back, but no one could give him back the time he lost or repay him for his mental anguish.

Why am I telling you these stories? To debunk the myth that if you are not a criminal, you will not get into trouble. Both John and J.J. were treated as though they were guilty until proven innocent. These horrors are not unique; in fact, they happen every day.

Now that we've established that even the most law-abiding citizens can be thrown in jail, we'll move on bail bonds and why it's so important to carry around that bail bondsman's number. Remember that until you are booked, you are not allowed a phone call to tell anyone where you are. Once you can, your first instinct may be to phone a friend or relative, but what if they don't know how to handle it? My point is that it's always good to be prepared. A bondsman is like a doctor; you never know when you will need one.

How Bail Bonds Work

As I've covered in previous chapters, once the charges are read to you, the clerk tells you whether you will have bail, and for how much. The next step is paying that bond so you can get the heck out of there, and unless you happen to have the cash on you, you will need someone to come down there and pay it for you. A bail bondsman will come to the jail and post bond so that, assuming the warrant search is clear, you can be processed out.

Now, the bondsman is taking a risk by putting up the money; after all, if you miss any of your court dates, the judge can revoke bail, and the bondsman would be out the full amount of the bond. That's why bondsmen charge a fee—usually ten percent of the bond amount—as a commission. That fee is non-refundable, even if the charges against you are ultimately dropped, but I can pretty much guarantee that you would rather pay the money than rot away in a cell until your trial date.

This does not mean that you will always need a bail bondsman. If you're arrested for a minor charge and can afford to post a cash bond, by all means do so. When your case is over, there are no fees due, and you will get all of your money back within a few weeks of the case disposition.

If, however, you are charged with a felony, the bond could be thousands of dollars, even tens of thousands, and there is a good chance that you don't have that kind of money just lying around. This is where the bail bondsman comes in. If your total bond is $25,000, he or she will post it and charge you $2,500. The bondsman will also take out a security against your assets in order to cover the cost of the bail. If you do not have enough assets, he/she might also take out securities against individuals willing to assist you, such as relatives and friends. For example, if your mother has agreed to help with your bail, she might have to put up her house as collateral; thereby, sharing in the risk.

The bondsman also has remedies in the event that you do not show up for trial. He/she can hire a bounty hunter to track you down; a bondsman also has the right to sue you for any monies given to the court for your bond. Finally, the bail bond agency is entitled to recover any unpaid money by claiming your assets or those owned by family and friends who are helping you.

As we saw in Chapter 2, there are certain circumstances under which an individual may be denied bail altogether. For example, if you are charged with a capital offense (one that carries the death penalty) or one that is punishable with life imprisonment.

Some examples of non-bondable offenses include:

- Armed kidnapping
- Armed robbery
- 1st or 2nd degree murder
- Burglary with an assault or battery
- Armed sexual battery
- Armed burglary
- Armed trafficking
- Lewd or lascivious battery on a child under 12

If you are charged with any of these offenses, you will be held without a bond until your first appearance or bond hearing unless the judge fails to find probable cause for the crime alleged. The good news is that even when bail has been denied, there are still ways in which you can pursue a bond.

One thing you can do is request and present an argument at what is known as an "Arthur Hearing". Think of the Arthur Hearing as a mini-trial. The prosecution presents its case in the form of live witness testimony and/or sworn affidavits. There is a high burden of proof placed upon the prosecution—it must establish that the proof of guilt is evident or the presumption is great. However, unlike a trial, prosecution can use hearsay to prove that the accused committed the crime for which he or she is charged.

The judge will listen to all the testimonies, read the affidavits, and review any other relevant evidence in order to determine whether the State of Florida has met its burden. During the second stage of the hearing, the judge determines whether the accused poses such a danger to the community that no pretrial release should be permitted.

Remember how relieved I was to learn that my arrest warrant did not have a "Nebbia" attached? That's because it would have made it much more difficult for me to get out of jail. Certain types of charges, whether filed by a state or the federal government, carry with them a Nebbia hold (aka Nebbia attachment) to your bond. Basically, it places another layer of bureaucracy and procedure upon which your release is conditioned.

What is a Nebbia Hold?

The Nebbia Hold is designed to ensure that the defendant is posting bond with funds obtained through legitimate and legal means, rather than from some criminal enterprise such as drug trafficking, money laundering or theft.

The term has its origins in the 1966 case U.S. v. Nebbia, which involved a defendant who was accused of trafficking large quantities of heroin. *U.S. v. Nebbia 357 F.2d 303 (C.A.N.Y. 1966).* Although that case was federal, several states have adopted it in their own courts. The State of Florida enacted Statute 903.046 for this purpose. The Nebbia court decided that whoever is posting the bond (whether it's the defendant or any family, friends and associates) must provide proof that the funds for posting the premium and collateral were acquired through legitimate means.

If a Nebbia Hold has been attached, a hearing may be required to decide the issue. Unlike an Arthur Hearing, the burden of proof will be on you, the defendant, during a Nebbia hearing, to prove the funds and/or collateral that you're putting up for bail come from a legitimate source. You can show this through testimony, accounting documents, tax returns, banking records, and business records. Then, assuming the court is satisfied (either through the hearing or an agreement between the attorneys and the judge), the court can remove the Nebbia hold and allow the defendant to bond out of jail.

On the other end of the spectrum are charges that do not require a bond at all. These are minor misdemeanors often referred to as "release on own reconnaissance" or "on reconnaissance" release (ROR). You won't need to post bond; however, you will still have to wait for the charges to be read before being processed out. This can take up to 24 hours.

How to Get Out of Jail Without Seeing a Judge

If you've ever watched *Law & Order* or other crime dramas, you might think that you have to go before a judge to get out of jail. While that is true with serious charges or probation violations, there are many cases when it is not. This is great news for anyone who wants to get out of jail immediately, rather than waiting a day or more to go before the bench.

Now, let's take a moment to review. Most jails have a standard bail schedule that specifies bail amounts for common crimes. When you're arrested, you have to wait until they call you to read the charge(s) and give you the amount of the bond. At that point, you can make your one phone call. If the bond is small, you can call a friend or relative and have them come to the jail and bail you out. If it's for a larger amount, you need to call your bail bondsman. He/she will come to the jail and post the bond so you can be processed out.

Regardless of who posts for you, time is of the essence. After a certain amount of time passes (especially at night), you will be taken back to the cell, where you'll sit until the next day when you can see a judge. This potentially adds another fifteen to twenty hours to your stay courtesy of the Florida penal system.

If for any reason you are unable to post bond, you will be scheduled to see a judge. This is called the First Appearance Hearing. By law, this must happen within twenty-four hours of your formal booking. At that hearing, the judge will reread the charges to you and advise you of your rights; he/she will also ask if you can afford an attorney and let you know that if not, you will be assigned a public defender. He/she will then review your current charges, as well as any previous criminal activity, and set an official bond. Please note that this may be a different amount than the one told to you by the booking clerk.

The obvious advantage of posting bail quickly is that you would be released without having to see the judge at all. This is not just a matter of wanting to get out of jail. It is within the judge's discretion to raise or lower the bond regardless of the amount you were already given by the clerk. You are at his/her mercy.

There is another, very important reason why you want to get out of jail before seeing a judge. Let's say you are out on bond from a previous arrest and you have now been arrested again. In most states, including Florida, being rearrested while out on bond is grounds for revoking your bail. However, this will not happen if you bond out prior to seeing the judge. This is one of those very important loopholes in the system that most defendants are not aware of. The jail only searches for outstanding warrants; they do not check to see whether you are already out on a bond.

Please note that these rules only apply to state charges. The federal system, which I discuss below, has few important differences.

The Federal Bail System

If you are arrested for one or more of them, the first thing to remember is that you should contact a bail bondsman who specializes in, and fully understands, the federal system. This is extremely important!

There are more than 4500 federal crimes, including the following:

- Any crimes concerning the Post Office, such as mailing illegal drugs or dangerous chemicals, mailing ransom notes, or vandalizing mailboxes.

- Any crimes that involve fraudulently accepting federal benefits such as welfare fraud, social security fraud, or forging a deceased person's signature on a social security check.

- Organized crime

- Importing illegal drugs or transporting them across state lines

- Kidnapping

- Bank robbery

- Counterfeiting

- Wire fraud

- Mail fraud
- Tax fraud
- Tax evasion
- Customs violations

A significant difference between the state and federal system is that when one is charged with a federal crime, they must go before a magistrate (judge). He or she will decide whether to release the defendant on their own reconnaissance or to give them restricted or unrestricted bail.

Restrictions on bail include things like limiting travel or forbidding it altogether; making sure the accused remains employed, or mandating medical and/or psychological evaluations. The amount of bail is also up to the magistrate. Unlike the state system, there is no bail schedule; however, it is usually a much higher amount than at the state level.

Also, if you are charged with a federal crime, expect to pay the bail bondsman a 15% fee, rather than 10% as on the state level.

In Chapter 4, I will discuss the arraignment process and what you can do to be prepared for your first court appearance.

CHAPTER 4
The Arraignment

Relieved as I was that I could post bail quickly and get out of the cell, I also knew that my ordeal had only just begun. Remember, our legal system is all about processes and procedures, and the next step in the criminal justice process is for the state to file formal charges. At this point, you may be thinking, *Wait a minute, wasn't I "formally charged" by the cops? How about when the clerk read me the charges and told me the bond amount? Wasn't I formally charged then?*

The answer is: not really. The cops did arrest you for committing an alleged crime; however, it is ultimately up to the state of Florida (or your state) to file the charges. It is the state, not the police, that determines the seriousness of the charges.

After your arrest, the state's attorney has the opportunity to review the law enforcement's account of the events leading to your arrest. Sometimes, the state's attorney will determine that the facts, as described by the officer, do not support the charges. If so, the state will file lesser charges (or none at all). On the other hand, they could also decide to charge you with crimes more serious than the police did. The decision often hinges upon whether the state's attorney believes he/she can get a conviction based on the evidence.

The wishes of the witnesses and victims of your alleged crimes are irrelevant. Sometimes, witnesses don't want to testify against you; sometimes, the victims do not want to file charges. That does not necessarily stop the case from moving forward. Florida state law gives the state's attorney the power to subpoena reluctant witnesses to testify; if they don't, they can be charged with contempt of court.

This is a good time to cover grand jury hearings. In the vast majority of cases, the prosecutor decides whether to proceed to trial; however, when it comes to a capital crime (one punishable by death), per the U.S. Constitution, a grand jury must be convened. A grand jury is a group of citizens empaneled by a federal or state court to investigate, report on and possibly accuse an individual of a crime. In doing so, they must determine whether probable cause exists that a crime has been committed and that the accused committed that crime. If such probable cause exists, the grand jury will return a "true bill" finding, which, when filed with the court, becomes an indictment and allows the state to move forward with a trial. If, on the other hand, the grand jury does not find probable cause, they will return a "no true bill" finding, and no indictment is handed down. The state can then continue its investigation and bring the case (along with any new incriminating evidence) before another grand jury at a later date.

The number of grand jurors depends on whether the case

is state or federal. It also varies from state to state and sometimes even within the state. In Florida, for example, a grand jury empaneled by a circuit court judge consists of 15-21 people, with 12 needed to indict. When the state is seeking an indictment for a multi-circuit crime, a statewide grand jury is empaneled by a judge of the Florida Supreme Court. A statewide grand jury has 18 members.

There are several important differences between a grand jury and a "petit" or trial jury. First, remember that unlike a trial jury, the grand jury is not charged with determining guilt or innocence, just whether the case should be brought to trial. Second, whereas at a trial each side gets an equal opportunity to present its case, only the prosecution has such an opportunity at a grand jury hearing. The state can subpoena witnesses, alleged victims and experts, and, given the investigatory capacity of the grand jury, the grand jurors can question these witnesses as well.

If a person called to testify before a grand jury refuses to answer a question, the grand jury will record the question and the refusal and investigate the surrounding circumstances. If, in the answering of the question, the witness would be incriminating him or herself, he or she cannot be compelled to answer. If there is no risk of self-incrimination (for example, the witness is merely protecting the accused), he or she must answer the question or be charged with contempt. Witnesses can also be convicted of perjury if they lie on the stand. An accused person cannot be forced to testify before the grand jury; he or she can voluntarily appear, but must clearly waive the right against self-incrimination. If he or she does not waive this right, any indictment will be null and void.

If you are called before a grand jury, as the accused or as a witness, be sure to bring your attorney with you. They cannot object on your behalf, but they can advise you on how to protect yourself.

Whether or not a grand jury is involved, the state only has a certain amount of time to file the charges. The length of time varies from state to state. In Florida, if the accused cannot afford to bond out of jail, the state has thirty days to file the formal charges. If it has not done so by the thirty-third day, the court will issue notice to the state and release the accused on his/her own recognizance unless the charged are filed on that day. The state may petition the court for an extension, but it must make a showing of good cause (i.e. they are still gathering valuable evidence). Even with the extension, however, charges must be filed no more than forty days from the date of arrest.

For those who were able to post bond, the state has a bit more time to file the charges—ninety days for misdemeanors and one-hundred eighty days for felonies. Once that time has passed, they cannot charge you; this is part of your right to a speedy trial, guaranteed under the Sixth Amendment to the Constitution.

Once the charges are filed, the next step is the arraignment. Those who have already bonded out of jail usually do not attend their arraignment. This is because their attorney, upon receiving the Notice of Arraignment, can file a Waiver of Appearance so that the accused does not have to face the humiliation of being charged in public. This is especially important when the case is getting media attention. The lawyer can also file a Motion for a Speedy Trial, a Motion for Discovery (which means the state has to turn over its evidence against the accused), and enter a plea on behalf of their client.

This is why it is so imperative that everyone who gets arrested has an attorney. As you have undoubtedly heard on hundreds of crime shows, "If you cannot afford one, the state will provide one without charge." Of course, you also have the right to represent yourself (also known as pro se), but as the saying goes, a person acting as their own attorney is a fool.

Those who have not bonded out will attend at the arraignment, which is before a judge. They can go with an attorney or without one; however, it is highly advisable that they are represented by counsel, as they will be asked to enter their plea. The accused will confirm for the court that he/she is the person named in the charges. He or she will then enter a plea of guilty, not guilty, or nolo contendere (no contest).

When someone pleads no contest, they are not admitting to guilt; they are simply saying they will not fight the charges. The effect of this plea varies depending upon the state and the nature of the charges. For example, it can help someone in defending a civil lawsuit that springs from the same circumstances as the criminal charge; however, it can potentially hurt them when looking for employment.

As far as the criminal court is concerned, pleading no contest also has the same effect as a conviction. If you plead guilty or no contest, the next step will be sentencing; in fact, depending upon the crime, it is possible that the judge will sentence you right then and there. If you plead not guilty, you will go to trial.

Our Arraignments

Josh, Peter and I all retained attorneys, who filed Waivers of Appearance so we would not have to attend our arraignments. After Josh's arraignment on March 28, 2013, I was shocked to learn that the state had filed the burglary and grand theft charges but dropped the charge of "obtaining property by false impersonation." As the state's entire case hinged on the fact that Josh had gone to the house and said he was "ABC Locksmith," I could not imagine how they would proceed against him without that charge.

Then I took a look at §810.02, Florida's rather vague burglary statute. Under that law, a person who enters a dwelling with the intent to commit a crime is guilty of a burglary. Usually, this intent is negated by an invitation; however Josh was invited in only because he had told the woman that he was from "ABC Locksmith." This lie, the state could argue, showed his intent to commit grand theft—the other crime he was charged with—once he gained entrance.

The defense would argue that regardless of what Josh said,

no burglary had occurred. Josh was in fact a locksmith, and he had performed the job to the woman's satisfaction. If anything, this was a case of two locksmiths fighting over a name—which, as I had been advised by three different attorneys before registering the names—was a civil matter. The defense would argue that Josh should never have ended up fighting for his freedom in criminal court.

All things considered, I didn't think the state had much of a case against him; at the end of the day, the woman had asked for a locksmith, and Josh showed up and did the job satisfactorily. It's not like he said he was a locksmith and turned out to be a plumber!

Once the defense explained what really happened, I felt it was unlikely that the jury would convict. Then, I tried to put myself in the mind of a juror; regardless of how frivolous you believe the charges to be, it is very extremely unnerving to consider how a group of strangers—each with his/her own backgrounds, perspectives, and biases—will interpret the facts. In fact, it is more than unnerving—it is truly terrifying.

As for the other count—grand theft—what exactly did Josh steal? As per the request of the customer (and sting participant), he had removed the lock, re-keyed it, and reinstalled the same lock. He then gave her a new set of keys. If you are wondering what he stole, you are not alone. In order for the state to prove its case, a jury would have to believe that Josh had stolen property worth more than $100 from the customer. He did leave the house with the woman's cash, which she had paid him for a job well done. Again, it seemed highly unlikely that a jury would convict him, but there are no guarantees.

On February 21, 2013, Peter, the second tech, was notified that his arraignment would be held on April 4, 2013. His attorney also filed a Waiver of Appearance and a demand for a speedy trial. Remember that, unlike Josh, Peter had not been charged with false personation, just the burglary and grand theft. At the arraignment, the state announced it was keeping both of those charges.

As with Josh, the state's case against Peter hinged on the fact that he had lied about being "ABC Locksmith" and that the customer would not have let him onto the premises otherwise. The grand theft charge was also very shaky. Peter had installed new locks for a customer; he had stolen nothing from the home, or as the statute states: "deprived the person use of their property."

Finally, it was my turn. After my arrest and speedy release from jail in August of 2013, I received notice that my arraignment would be held on October 10th. By September 3rd, my attorney had already waived my appearance and filed for a speedy trial.

As with Josh, the state attorney's office dropped the "obtaining property by false personation" charge against me; however, the other two charges more than made up for it. For using names similar to other locksmiths, I was being charged with "money laundering" and "organized scheme to defraud"!

If you're thinking these sound like very serious charges,

you're right. They are both second degree-felonies, and if convicted, I could be sent to jail for fifteen years. Imagine receiving that kind of sentence for putting up a few websites to attract business. Rapists and murderers often receive less. Not to mention the fact that my websites were completely different than those of the other companies and contained a disclosure stating that were not the other companies in question. Logically, I knew that this whole thing was ridiculous; however, logic goes out the window when you are the one going to trial.

The wording of the statutes under which I was charged made it all the more terrifying. Under Florida's "organized scheme to defraud" statute, the state does not have to prove that the so-called victims lost any money; they only have to prove that, in some way, I misrepresented myself or my company. Basically, if the jury did not like the way I did my advertising, they could convict me.

That was not the worst of it. We usually think of money laundering as being committed by some drug kingpin or organized crime family; however, the Florida Money Laundering Act (§896.101) is much broader than that. The act clearly states that if you make money from an illegal activity, then you are guilty of money laundering. If you are guilty of organized scheme to defraud, you made money from an illegal activity. That meant that if the jury convicted me on the organized scheme to defraud, they would automatically have to convict me for money laundering! Suddenly, my entire life was at risk.

As I had contended from the beginning, this was a civil

matter and not a criminal case at all. The police officer who had conducted the "investigation" and made the arrests was trying to protect the locksmith company that did the work for the town of Palm Beach. This case was about nothing more than teaching me a lesson; I had to admit, if nothing else, he had certainly accomplished his mission.

Chapter 5
Guilty Until Proven Innocent

As Americans, we are taught from childhood that we are innocent until proven guilty—this is one of the cornerstones of our legal system and has often distinguished us from other nations as a leader of the free world. However, it is my opinion that although this is true in theory, it is not always true in the execution (no pun intended). In fact, in many ways, people are treated as though they are guilty until proven innocent. While the development of DNA testing has freed many wrongly convicted people and prevented the wrongful convictions of others, there are many people who continue to suffer through the effects of being in the wrong place at the wrong time, or simply being the wrong race. I am speaking here from personal experience, not just because of my own legal wrangles, but because of people I have known.

Back when I was living in New York, I had good friend named Joe. People in the neighborhood always knew that Joe was going somewhere. He was a nice guy, a great student, and highly motivated to succeed. By the time he was in his early twenties, Joe had landed a good job with an engineering firm, earning $75,000—an excellent salary in the 1970s. He was also newly married, and he and his wife had bought a house in Brooklyn. They had their whole lives ahead of them, and it promised to be a very good life indeed.

Unfortunately, Joe was about to find out that everything could be taken from him in the blink of an eye.

One night, around 11 p.m., he was walking home from a movie. As he turned down a dark street not far from his home, two police cars roared to a stop next to him. Joe didn't think much of it, and why would he? He was just minding his own business.

He noticed a young woman sitting in the first car. Her window was down, and she seemed to be staring at Joe. He heard one of the cops say something to her, and she replied, "Yes, that's the guy." Then, before he had a chance to say anything, Joe was slammed to the ground by two police officers.

As he lay face down on the sidewalk, the cops informed him that the woman in the car had just identified him as the man who raped her an hour earlier. She claimed he had forced her into an alley, where he sexually assaulted her. The physical description she gave the police was certainly close, right down to the green jacket that Joe was wearing.

The cops handcuffed him, threw him in the back of the second police car, and sped off to the local precinct. If you think this is terrifying, just wait—Joe's nightmare had only begun.

Although he was no attorney, Joe certainly knew that

sexual assault was a major felony. On the other hand, he knew he hadn't done anything wrong, so how far could the cops take it? They would question him, realize he really had been at the movies, and let him go.

After four brutal hours of interrogation, however, he realized that it didn't matter what he said; the cops believed the victim's identification. Sure enough, they charged him with kidnapping and aggravated rape. He was then transported to the main jail and booked. Given the charges, needless to say there was a NO Bond Hold.

Remember that Joe was picked up off the street and taken straight to jail. For all his wife and parents knew, he had just disappeared into thin air. It wasn't until twenty-four hours later that he was permitted to call his relatives and let them know what was going on. They were shocked, of course, and jumped to do the only thing they could at this point: contact an attorney. Upon hearing the circumstances, the lawyer told Joe that due to the seriousness of the charges and the legal work involved, he would have pay a $50,000 retainer; if the case went to trial, the total cost of his defense would be $100,000.

Although Joe was on the path to success, he was just starting out and did not have anywhere near $50,000. He had to borrow $25,000 against his house, and his parents took out a mortgage on their own home in order to come up with the other half. You should note that Joe had not even been officially charged by the state yet—there is no proof that he did anything—but he was already in jail, without a bond, and out $50,000. While he might have been technically considered "innocent", he was certainly being treated like the guiltiest man alive. You should also note that once you give an attorney a retainer, it is very rare that you'll get any of that money back, even if the case is down-filed or dismissed.

Thirty days later, he was arraigned in a Brooklyn courthouse, where the state did formally file the kidnapping and aggravated rape charges against him. At this time, the judge set bail at $250,000. As I explained in the chapter on bail bonds, he would have to come up with 10% of that—another $25,000—in order to bond out of jail. If you're thinking this is a lot of money, remember that in the 1970s, it was a ton of money.

Fortunately, his mother, with the help of three close friends, was able to raise the money. However, given the large bond amount, the bail bondsman also required some collateral. That meant Joe's mother also had to put up some stocks and real estate to secure the bond. It took another five days for that paperwork to go through, and finally, Joe was released from jail.

By that time, he had been out of work for nearly two months, and he and his family were out $75,000.

Even worse, he still had the trial hanging over his head. His attorney was scrambling to find exculpatory evidence and build a defense. Sure enough, six months later, and just fifteen days before Joe's trial was to begin, a similar attack occurred in the same Brooklyn neighborhood. This time, they caught the suspect running from the scene of the crime; the victim had also fought back, leaving scratch marks on him. After the man was arrested, the first victim—the one who had pointed the finger at Joe—was called to a lineup that included both Joe and the new suspect. The victim took one look at the row of men and immediately and positively identified, not Joe, but the new suspect! Given this development, as well as other details that turned up during the course of the investigation, the New York District Attorney concluded that Joe was not the one who had attacked the first victim. Within ten days, all charges against him were dismissed.

Obviously, this was an enormous relief to Joe and his family. If convicted of the rape and kidnapping charges, he could have been sentenced from fifteen years to life in state prison.

While he was thrilled to be free, his nightmare was far from over. He was still out the $50,000 retainer, as his attorney had worked on the case for over six months. The bail was released to the bondsman; however, he would keep $25,000 of that as his commission for posting the bond.

Joe had lost more than money; he had also lost half a year of his life—more than a month behind bars and several months terrified that he would spend the rest of his life in prison.

To make matters even worse, he had lost his job while out on bond. Due to the seriousness of the charges, the firm where he had shown so much promise now considered him a liability. One could hardly blame them for not wanting a suspected rapist working there. The real tragedy of it is that even once the charges were dropped, the cloud of suspicion continued to hang over his head. Remember, there was no DNA testing back then to definitively prove that he wasn't the culprit; as far as anyone knew, Joe might have gotten off on a technicality. For this reason, he was also unable to find another job, and when he could no longer pay his mortgage, the bank was forced to foreclose on his house. Even his wife was never completely convinced of his innocence. The ordeal stretched their marriage to the breaking point, and they eventually divorced. Joe had never had so much as a traffic ticket; all he had was the lousy luck of walking on the wrong street at the wrong time and wearing the wrong color jacket.

Right now, you may be thinking that this is a horrifying story, but what does it have to do with my locksmith case? My answer is: everything. Because while Joe was charged with a violent attack, I was charged with a white collar crime; and although his case was one of mistaken identity, and I was arrested for something that should have been a civil matter, we were both wrongfully charged, and we were both treated as though we were guilty until proven innocent.

We were both facing serious jail time, and we both spent tens of thousands of non-refundable dollars in bail bonds and legal fees to make sure that didn't happen. Still, that did not guarantee a positive outcome. The awful truth is that if a second woman had not been raped, Joe would have either gone to trial or been forced to make a deal with the prosecution. In my case, I had to make arrangements to avoid being tried for a crime I should never have been charged with. But I will discuss this issue later in the chapter on trials and plea bargains.

What did Joe get for all the trouble he had gone through? A curt "sorry" from the state's attorney. This does not even begin to cover all his losses—not the least of which were in his good name. Unlike Florida, New York does not seal or expunge records; therefore whenever someone runs a criminal background check (i.e. for a job application), they see aggravated rape and kidnapping on his record. Sure, it shows it was dismissed, but not that he was wrongly charged to begin with. Would you hire him?

My point is that the injustice continued long after the charges against Joe were dismissed; furthermore, I believe the state should have made him whole for all he'd suffered. They should have paid him back for the $50,000 retainer he had given the attorney and the $25,000 he had given to the bail bondsmen. They should have also compensated him for the loss of his job and his home. Finally, they should have made a public statement that he had been wrongly charged and that the victim had identified the real rapist.

With the way the system currently operates, even if you win the trial or the criminal case is dismissed, you are still the loser. Even if you do not go to prison, the state can demolish your life then leave you to pick up the pieces—if you can. That's why I believe the criminal system should work as the civil system does.

Civil Cases

If you remember from chapter one, I was advised by three different attorneys that registering names similar to those of other locksmith companies was a civil, not criminal, matter. In other words, if the other companies did not like what I was doing, they could sue me civilly in an attempt to stop me from using those names and/or for restitution for any business they lost as a result of my actions. Civil cases are all about money; no one ever goes to jail because they lost such a suit.

If you do lose, however, you will have to pay the winner, not only the amount of the judgment he was awarded; you will also pay all court costs and attorney's fees. If you do not pay, the plaintiff can try to get a writ to seize your assets. In most states, you are allowed certain exemptions from the writ—things like your primary residence, as well as any IRA accounts, traditional or Roth. Most retirement plans and social security benefits are also exempt from such judgments. Although you cannot always protect yourself from being sued, at least you know that you won't go to jail or lose your home.

Another great thing about civil cases is that if you successfully defend yourself against a suit, the court will usually award you court costs and reasonable attorney's fees. That protects people, to some degree, from the frivolous lawsuits; you will not be out the tens of thousands of dollars it took to successfully defend yourself.

If criminal cases were handled this way, you could bet the state would not be so quick to file charges. In Joe's case, for example, the cops might have gone to the movie theater where Joe claimed to be in order to verify his alibi.

In my case, the state's attorney would have certainly declined to file against me; the matter would have stayed where it should've been—in civil court.

If we are truly a country that treats the accused as "innocent until proven guilty," then the criminal court system should operate similarly to the civil system. The system as it currently operates is patently unfair, as only the wealthy or well-to-do can afford to pay the bond and attorneys' fees for a good defense. Others, like Joe, are broken financially, while the poor wind up with less than stellar representation. They often end up in jail or take a plea bargain even if they have not committed the crime.

Our jails are filled with such people; one must only look at those who have been exonerated through the use of DNA testing. To date, 316 people in the U.S. have been cleared post-conviction. These innocent citizens were jailed for serious crimes often as a result of the overzealousness of police and prosecutors, as well as racial and socioeconomic inequities that have long been played out in the criminal justice system. In fact, studies show that 70% of those exonerated by DNA were persons of color. They also show that the wrongfully convicted spent an average of 13.6 years in prison. There were also eighteen people, listed below, who were sitting on death row for crimes they did not commit.

Kirk Bloodsworth served eight years in Maryland prison—including two years on death row—for a murder and rape he didn't commit before he was exonerated in 1993.

Rolando Cruz, and his co-defendant Alejandro Hernandez, served more than 10 years on Illinois death row for a murder they didn't commit before DNA testing proved both men innocent in 1995.

Verneal Jimerson and Dennis Williams were sentenced to death in the infamous Ford Heights Four case in Illinois for a pair of 1978 murders they didn't commit. Jimerson was cleared in 1995 after a decade on death row and Williams served more than 17 years on death row before he was freed in 1996.

Robert Miller spent 9 years on Oklahoma's death row for a murder and rape he didn't commit before he was cleared by DNA testing in 1998.

Ron Williamson spent a decade on Oklahoma's death row for a murder he didn't commit before DNA testing secured by the Innocence Project proved him innocent in 1999. His co-defendant, Dennis Fritz, was sentenced to life and spent 11 years in prison before DNA cleared him as well.

Ronald Jones, an Innocence Project client, served a decade on Illinois death row for a murder and rape he didn't commit before DNA testing proved his innocence and led to his release in 1999.

Earl Washington, a Virginia man with limited mental capacity, was sentenced to death after he allegedly confessed to committing a 1982 murder he didn't commit. He served a decade on death row, once coming within nine days of execution before receiving a stay. He served a total of 17 years behind bars before DNA testing obtained by the Innocence Project cleared him in 2000.

Frank Lee Smith died of cancer on Florida's death row after serving 14 years for a murder and rape he didn't commit. He was cleared by DNA testing obtained by the Innocence Project 11 months after his death.

Charles Irvin Fain served more than 17 years on death row in Idaho for a murder and rape he didn't commit before DNA testing proved his innocence in 2001.

Ray Krone served a decade in Arizona prison—including four years on death row—for a murder and rape he didn't commit before DNA testing proved his innocence in 2002.

Nicholas Yarris served more than 21 years on Pennsylvania's death row before DNA testing proved his innocence and led to his release in 2003.

Ryan Matthews served five years on Louisiana's death row for a murder he didn't commit before he was exonerated by DNA testing in 2004. His co-defendant, Travis Hayes, was sentenced to life in prison and served eight years before he was cleared in 2007.

Curtis McCarty served 21 years in Oklahoma prison—including nearly 18 years on death row—for a murder he didn't commit before DNA tests secured by the Innocence Project led to his exoneration in 2007. He was convicted twice and sentenced to death three times based on forensic misconduct.

Kennedy Brewer, an Innocence Project client, served 15 years behind bars—including seven years on death row—for a murder and sexual assault he didn't commit before DNA testing from 2001 finally led to his exoneration in 2008.

Michael Blair served 13 years on death row for a murder he didn't commit before DNA testing obtained by his lawyers at the Innocence Project proved his innocence and led to his exoneration in 2008.

Damon Thibodeaux spent 15 years on death row in Louisiana before he was exonerated in 2012. A prosecution expert who aided in the reinvestigation of his case concluded that the threat of the death penalty contributed to why he falsely confessed to the murder of his cousin.

Despite all of the procedures and evidentiary rules designed to protect the innocent, these men were wrongly convicted and lost years of their lives. In all likelihood, they would have been executed if not for DNA testing and organizations like the Innocence Project, which are committed to freeing the wrongly accused.

To make matters worse, Florida is moving further away from protecting the rights of the accused. It used to be that in order to be convicted of a crime, the prosecution had to prove two things: a guilty act and a guilty mind. There had to be an intent on the part of the accused to break the law. While this is still true for serious felonies like rape, murder and burglary, there are other crimes for which lawmakers are trying to erase the intent requirement.

For example, the Shelton case, which started out as a drug matter but became a much larger issue; namely, can the rules be changed so that burden of proof falls to the defendant to show he did not intend to break the law?

The defendant in Shelton was convicted of the possession and delivery of cocaine. He appealed his conviction, stating that the judge's instructions to the jury had removed the intent requirement. Shelton also pointed out that in Staples v. United States, the U.S. Supreme Court had held that a "strict liability" crime (one that requires no intent), must have a slight penalty and a slight stigma attached to it. It must involve an item or substance that was clearly illegal (such as a bomb or other weapon), as opposed to a powder that the defendant may or may not have known was an illegal drug. As Shelton had been sentenced to 18 years for possession of a powdery substance, this case did not follow legal precedent.

Shelton won his appeal in a federal district court in Florida; however, the U.S. Eleventh Circuit Court of Appeals threw out the district court's decision. Shelton's conviction—and very lengthy sentence—would stand.

This case is so important because it demonstrates Florida's current legal and political climate. It also explains why many innocent people choose to accept a plea bargain—even if it means doing time for a crime they did not commit—rather than going to trial. I will get into that further in the next chapter.

CHAPTER 6
Plea or Trial

The next step, usually within several weeks of the arraignment, will be an offer of a plea bargain. When a plea bargain is in place, the state's attorney makes a promise to the defendant that, in exchange for a guilty or no contest plea, he/she will get either reduced or no jail time. The defendant may also be required to provide testimony against others; for example, if he/she had co-conspirators. The rationale is that a plea deal saves both the state and the defendant the time and money involved with a trial.

There are two kinds of plea deals in Florida—a charge bargain and a sentence bargain. With a charge bargain, the defendant is permitted to plead to a lesser charge, or, if he/she has been charged with more than one crime, the lesser charges may be dropped in exchange for a guilty plea on the main charge.

Let's say you are arrested for burglary and suspected of several others. When the cops search your home for stolen goods, they find an unlicensed firearm. They may offer to drop the gun charge in exchange for your guilty plea on the burglary.

The other kind of plea bargain—the sentence bargain—

means that if you plead guilty to the charges, you will be given less jail time, and you will know what the sentence is at the time of the pleading.

For example, let's say you've been charged with rape. The maximum sentence if convicted is twenty years to life, but the prosecutor offers you a sentence of five years if you plead guilty. This is what was offered to Robert, whose case we'll discuss in a bit.

If you are guilty of the crime(s) you've been charged with, a plea bargain is a great deal. If you are innocent—not so much. At this point, you might be thinking, *but why in the world would an innocent person plead guilty?* The answer, in a word, is fear—fear that if wrongly convicted, you could spend the better part of your life in jail; depending on where you live, you may even get the death penalty! After all, you were wrongly arrested and wrongly charged, so your faith in the justice system may already be faltering, and rightfully so.

Most people don't realize how often this happens. According to statistics, only five to ten percent of criminal cases actually go to trial; the rest are disposed of through plea bargains. Even more disturbing is the fact that twenty percent of exonerated persons plead guilty as part of a plea bargain. Some researchers claim that thousands—even tens of thousands – of innocent people are sitting in jail as a result. Even those who do not get jail time will have the crime on their record, ruining their reputations and even preventing them from getting employment. Remember my friend Joe who was accused of rape? Even though the real perpetrator was eventually caught, that arrest ruined his professional and personal life.

This is not to say that plea bargains are not valid or important. They keep the court system moving. Can you imagine if everyone charged with a crime went to trial? The justice system would grind to a halt, and the prisons would have to start releasing people early to make room for more serious criminals.

This chapter will discuss why it can be to your benefit to take a plea even if you DID NOT commit the crime. The unfortunate truth is that if you are offered a plea deal and refuse it, you most likely will receive jail time even if you're a first-time offender. In a bit, I will give two tragic examples of this.

But first, a word of advice for FIRST TIME OFFENDERS who DID commit the crime they've been charge with: TAKE THE DEAL. You can bargain with the state to let you plea to a lesser charge, and if you are a non-violent offender, chances are you'll be given a pretty good deal.

In a lot of jurisdictions, including Florida, you can ask the state to give you what is called an "Adjudication Withheld" on the plea. This means that even if you are charged with a felony and plead guilty or no contest, you will not be considered a convicted felon. Remember though that this is not available in all jurisdictions; also, some states require a waiting period to apply for certain professional licenses even after adjudication is withheld. You must check with your attorney, as well as any applicable licensing bodies.

Another option for first time offenders is "Pretrial Diversion". Essentially, this is a twelve-month probation—if you don't get in any trouble and comply with all the terms of the deal, all charges will be dismissed, leaving you with no criminal record. I will discuss this further in the next chapter.

Now, back to those who are *not* guilty of the crime. Let's say, for example, that you rear end someone with your car, and that person is killed. Even though it was an accident, there is good chance that you will be charged with vehicular homicide, which, in the state of Florida, carries a sentence of fifteen years in jail.

Sounds excessive, right? There was no criminal intent, no intoxication, yet, if convicted, the judge can throw the book at you. Suddenly, you are at risk of losing everything, and you are terrified. Then the prosecutor comes along and "generously" offers you a plea agreement. If you plead guilty to the vehicular manslaughter, you will "only" have to serve five years. Still excessive for an accident, in my opinion, but at least you can see the light at the end of the tunnel. Your attorney may even be advising you to take the deal, particularly if he/she is an overworked, underpaid Legal Aid attorney.

Since you know this it was truly an accident, you say, "No way! I'm not spending five years in prison!" But if you're like most people, you're not aware that if you turn down the plea bargain and are later convicted by a jury, the judge will not give you the five years you were offered—he or she will give you ten years, if not the maximum. This is true, even if you have never been arrested in your life.

Don't believe it? Well, it actually happened to Robert, a man from Boca Raton, Florida. On the evening of June 4th, 1999, Robert, an insulin-dependent diabetic, was driving west on Yamato Road when he started feeling ill. Knowing he had to get home as quickly as possible, he sped up. He was going twenty miles over the speed limit as he went over an overpass and plowed into another car, which was carrying six retirees from the Whisper Walk Community. All six were killed.

The Palm Beach Country State Attorney's Office filed six counts of manslaughter against him. When the story broke, some said Robert deserved to go to jail forever; those who knew Robert disagreed, saying he was a kind family man who had never been in trouble in his life.

A successful advertising executive, Robert had the resources to hire Richard Lubin, one of the best criminal attorneys in Florida. He was able to bond out of jail until his trial. However, approximately a year after the accident, the prosecutor offered him a deal: five years in prison for all six counts. Robert refused that plea; he had not been under the influence of any drugs or alcohol, and he had not been on a joyride. He just could not believe a jury of his peers would send him to jail for an accident. That decision would turn out to be a colossal mistake.

At trial, his lawyer argued that the diabetes had caused a dangerous drop in blood pressure, which in turn induced a trancelike state. Therefore, Robert was impaired as he sped down the street that night. The attorney also asserted that the authorities were under pressure to make someone pay for the six deaths, even if it had been an accident. Robert was being scapegoated to avoid a public outcry.

After an eight-day trial that cost the taxpayers thousands of dollars in expert witness and attorney fees, the jury took only three hours to convict him of all six counts of manslaughter. The jury didn't buy the defense's medical defense or its claim of sloppy investigating.

"No matter what, he was speeding, and he did go through a red light and did crash into this car," one juror remarked. "We didn't have reasonable doubt."

Robert had assumed that the six people on the jury would look at the accident from his point of view, when, in actuality, they sympathized with the families of the dead. This is the thing about juries—you never know which way they are going to go.

One juror did argue that he should be acquitted, but the others wore her down until she changed her vote. Due to the number of deaths involved, Robert could have been sentenced to life in prison. One of the victim's relatives advocated for anywhere between ten and thirty years. He got his wish; Robert was sentenced to fifteen years by Palm Beach County Circuit Judge Edward Garrison.

"Mr. Robert, no matter how much time you have left on this Earth and no matter where you spend it, at least you will have the time to reflect on your life. Say goodbye to your friends and loved ones," Garrison said. "That luxury was not afforded to the six innocent people whose lives you snuffed out in June 1999."

Despite this, the judge called it one of the most difficult decisions in his more than twenty years on the bench. Robert's attorney had asked he that receive house arrest along with probation.

He managed to stay out of jail for several more years while he went through the appeals process. On July 5, 2007, eight years after the accident, he had lost his last appeal. He was immediately taken into custody to begin serving out his fifteen years.

Perhaps the most tragic part of Robert's story is that the jury was never told that he could get such a severe sentence. In fact, jurors in Florida criminal cases are never told the possible sentences awaiting criminal defendants; this is withheld intentionally, so it won't influence their interpretation of the facts. This is understandable in some cases; however, when it comes to people like Robert, it is patently unfair. The jury foreman has since said that if the jurors were aware of the strict sentence awaiting Robert under state guidelines, then the chances of conviction would have been "nil". Unfortunately, the appeals court did not feel the same way.

This is an example of what could happen to anyone who rejects a plea bargain. As of 2014, Robert is still rotting away in a Florida prison. Had he accepted the state's offer, he would have been out of jail by the time he was 48. Now he will be in jail until 2016, when he is nearly 60 years old!

Cases like Robert's happen more often than we know. In

fact, they have become all too commonplace. "An Offer You Can't Refuse", a report published by Human Rights Watch, reveals the unethical practices of prosecutors against defendants who refuse plea bargains. According to the report, only three percent of U.S. drug defendants in federal cases chose to go to trial in 2012. The alleged reason for this is that prosecutors threatened them with more serious charges and longer sentences if they did not take whatever deal was on the table.

Many have heard of the mandatory sentencing of New York's Rockefeller Drug Laws, which human rights advocates refer to as "Draconian". In 1985, one man learned just how horrible they were after he refused a three-year plea deal and was sentenced fifteen years to life.

The man was arrested after a friend offered to pay him $500 to deliver a package. The friend neglected to tell him that the package contained four ounces of cocaine. Although the prosecutor knew he was not a drug dealer, he still pushed forward with the case. He also offered the defendant a plea deal of three years, and when the defendant opted to exercise his constitutional right to a trial, he was convicted and sentenced to fifteen years behind bars. While in jail, he tried to commit suicide; he was also stuck with a knife and beaten with a pipe.

The worst part of his ordeal is that it destroyed his relationship with his daughter. She was only seven-years old when he went to prison, and the visits were extremely traumatic for her. Eventually, she stopped coming to see him entirely.

As the above stories show, judges routinely hand out stiff sentences, even to first-time offenders, simply because they exercised their constitutional right to a trial.

I contend that before taking the bench, each judge should have to go through the system, even if it's just for a day. If judges had to spend a night in jail, go through the arrest, booking and bail processes, then lie in a filthy cell for a night, they would have a clearer picture of what they are doling out to others. I bet they wouldn't be so fast to send someone to jail for a minor crime.

In fact, around the time I started writing this book, two Broward County Judges were arrested and had to do just that.

In November 2013, Boca Raton police responded to reports of an erratic driver on West Palmetto Road. When they pulled the car over, they were shocked to find Judge Cynthia Imperato behind the wheel. Imperato was slurring her words when she refused to take a breath test; however, the officer could smell liquor on her breath. The following videos, captured by the cops' dashcam, clearly show that this judge doesn't practice what she preaches.

http://www.youtube.com/watch?v=TyJcWhlPFW4

http://www.youtube.com/watch?v=UwCHPM4zzlM

Here are some interesting facts on Judge Cynthia Imperato:

While she was under prosecution for a crime, she was allowed to hand down a death sentence on November 7

2014. The issue here is not whether or not the defendant deserved the sentence. No person under prosecution for a crime can serve on any jury; however, the rules seem to differ for a judge.

On top of that, most people take a plea because they are afraid that if they are found guilty at trial, they will certainly be sent to jail. After all, they took up the court's time and exercised their right to a trial. Again, the rules are different for a sitting judge. She was offered a plea deal for her case of a six month suspension of her driver's license and 12 months of probation, and she turned it down!

She went to trial, and on December 19, 2014, she was convicted of both charges of DUI & reckless driving, and the prosecutor asked for a minimum of 30 days in jail. Did she get that? NO. Her sentence was 20 days house arrest, 12 months probation, $2531.00 in fines & court costs, and a 12 month suspension of her driver's license. She must attend 2 AA meetings a week. Not bad for losing at trial! Almost the same as a plea bargain.

It should be noted that at this time, as this book is going to print, she is appealing this conviction. She is still very unhappy with the outcome, and she is still a sitting judge at this time! My point here is that everyone would go to trial if they would get almost the same outcome as the plea deal with NO jail time.

Less than six months later, another Broward County Judge Gisele Pollack was also arrested on DUI charges.

Police arrested her after she hit another car, causing a neck injury to the driver. Like Imperato, her breath smelled of alcohol. Pollack had run a misdemeanor drug court for several years.

Now that these two judges have gone through the system, one would hope they'll be more understanding of how a defendant feels and more likely to show a little mercy, especially when the crime is a minor one.

Pollack was booked into the county jail at about 1:30 a.m. and released a few hours later. However, given her past history with drug and alcohol abuse and a subsequent "meltdown" in court, she was put on leave.

http://www.local10.com/news/broward-drug-court-judge-arrested-for-dui/25772854

It should be noted that both judges did not have to post any bond and were released on their own recognizance (ROR).

Remember, the rules are different for a judge!

Should you ever be in the position of having to take a plea agreement, you will be forced to answer several questions. Do not take these questions lightly, because if the judge does not like your answer, he or she will not accept your plea.

First, they will ask, "Are you pleading guilty because you are in fact guilty?"

You had better say yes!

Then they will ask, "Did anyone in any way force you to

accept this plea?"

You had better say NO!

Then they will ask, "Do you realize by taking this plea, you are giving up your rights to a jury trial and present evidence in your defense?"

You had better say yes!

They will then say, "With all that considered, are you entering this guilty plea because you are in fact guilty?"

You had better say yes!

At that point, you might be asked to allocate (admit, in detail) to the crime. This depends on the case.

If, like so many other defendants, you have been coerced into taking a plea, you may be tempted to say to the judge, "Yes, I feel I am being forced to take this plea, because if I don't, and if I exercise my right to a jury trial and lose, you will throw the book at me. So, yes, I am being forced!"

As much as you want to, don't ever say that to a judge; they will refuse the plea deal. This is the main reason why even innocent people sometimes accept a plea. Let's face it, the system is stacked against you. Even if you win at trial, you have still incurred major expenses and lost weeks, months or maybe years of your life. Even if you win, you lose, and the state knows that.

The next chapter will cover everything you should know about probation, including the different types of probation, the rights you forfeit during the period, and ways in which you can get an early termination.

CHAPTER 7
Probation and
How it Works

As we saw in the previous chapter, it is very common for someone charged with a crime to be offered a plea agreement. While even violent or repeat offenders may be offered less jail time in return for their no contest or guilty plea, those accused of a non-violent or white-collar crime may be allowed to avoid jail altogether, especially if they are first time offenders. However, regardless of the crime or the criminal record of the accused, the plea agreement will most likely include a probation period.

Probation is the criminal justice system's way of saying, "We don't think you have to be locked up, but we do need to keep tabs on you to make sure you stay out of trouble." It is essentially a game of trust. Probation can be offered in lieu of jail time, or the probation period may begin once the person has finished serving their prison sentence. You can just imagine how relieved a defendant would be to hear that they may be given an offer of probation; it means they are essentially free to live their lives as before. However, there are still things everyone should know before accepting an offer of probation.

The first thing to remember is that there are different kinds of probation, the most common type being Supervised Probation, which is overseen by the Department of Corrections. Usually, the term of Supervised Probation is between one and three years for misdemeanors and three to ten years for felonies.

Probation also carries with it certain conditions—things you agree to do or refrain from doing for the duration of the probation period. Most of these conditions are considered standard regardless of what state you live in or the circumstances of your case. However, it is important to keep in mind that probation will vary from state to state. As with every aspect of your case, you must check with your attorney to make sure you understand the particulars. Below is a list of those standard conditions that will be included in the terms of your Supervised Probation. Remember, if you do not follow the rules, you can be sent back to jail for the entire sentence that was originally set forth for that crime.

- Regularly check in with your probation officer. In most cases, this means going down to the probation office on a monthly or even weekly basis (your probation officer will let you know how often). You will affirm for him or her that you are complying with the terms of your probation (namely, keeping out of trouble). After you've complied with these terms for some time, he or she may tell you that you don't have to come as often or that you may check in by phone.

- Let them check in with you. When you are on Supervised Probation, the probation officer can come to your home or other places you frequent to make sure you are complying with the terms. This is non-negotiable; you must give him/her access to your life. If you think this sounds inconvenient, you are right. However, it is better than sitting in a jail cell!

- Hold down a job. As long as you are physically able, you must be gainfully employed.

- Live at a specified residence. The probation officer must have your address on file (remember, the point of Supervised Probation is to keep tabs on you). You must provide the probation officer with your address, and if you move, you have to let them know.

- DO NOT BREAK ANY LAWS! This is a big one, obviously, and it involves even minor infractions. While on probation, you must be on your best behavior in every regard. Let's say for example, that you are out with your friends for a couple of drinks (if you're even allowed to drink on probation), and let's say there is a guy in the bar who's had a few too many and is looking for trouble. No matter how he taunts you, you must keep your cool, because getting in a bar fight could be a violation of your probation.

- Choose your friends wisely. While on probation, you cannot associate with people who are involved with criminal activities. This can be a particularly tough one, especially if your circle of friends includes people who are not completely on the up and up. It won't matter if you're an innocent bystander, if you are hanging out with people who break the law, you are violating your probation.

- Pay up. The terms of your probation will probably include some sort of financial obligations. In addition to staying current with your child support and other responsibilities to your legal dependents, you must also pay any court-ordered restitution, court costs and attorney fees; you may even be required to pay for medical treatment you received while incarcerated.

- Do your duty. While on probation, you may be required to perform community service such as volunteering for a charity or doing some sort of manual labor.

- No packing. While on probation you cannot possess, carry, or own a firearm or any other weapon unless given express consent by your probation officer.

- Stay sober. While on probation, you are not allowed to drink to excess (if at all) or possess any drugs or narcotics not prescribed by a physician. You must submit to random testing to make sure you're staying clean. In addition, you cannot knowingly go to places where these substances are illegally sold, used or dispensed.

- Submit to a swab. People on probation must provide a DNA sample to the Florida Department of Law Enforcement (FDLE), which they will then add to their database. They are doing this so that if you are accused of a future crime, they can compare your sample to any DNA found at the scene. The good news is, this DNA can also exonerate you.

- Strike a pose. You must allow the FDLE to take a photo of you for their records. This will be posted to the probation's website during the term of supervision.

- The open door policy. When you accept an offer of Supervised Probation, you are agreeing to random, warrantless searches of your home, motor vehicle, and self. The probation officer can show up at your home or business at any time without prior notice.

Sometimes, depending on the nature of the crime, your probation will have extra conditions, such as community service, fines and/or restitution. If you are on probation for a drug or alcohol-related offense, you will not be allowed to consume any alcohol; you will also be required to take regular urine tests to make sure you're staying clean. Failing or refusing to take a drug test is a VOP (violation of probation) and will most likely mean you are going (or returning) to jail.

If for any reason you think you might not be able to comply with these conditions, then by all means, do not accept a plea offer that includes probation. Of course, if your probation term follows your release from prison, you have no choice unless you want to land back behind bars.

As I mentioned earlier, there are different types of probation. While Supervised Probation has a laundry list of rules and regulations, Administration Probation is much less restrictive. This type of probation is usually only offered to people charged with misdemeanors; however, those charged with a felony may also be given Administrative Probation as a reward for complying with the terms of their Supervised Provision for a certain amount of time.

Those on Administrative Probation do not have to visit the Probation Office; they simply mail in a report each month. As long as they stay out of trouble, everything is fine. And unlike Supervised Probation, you are free to travel without permission from the Probation Officer. In most cases, the Probation Officer will NOT visit you at home.

The rules for probation may seem simple; however, they do involve a forfeiture of some of the constitutional rights most of us take for granted. The important thing to remember is that while these rules may be inconvenient and even humiliating, they are certainly preferable to incarceration. If you forget this, you will join the large number of defendants who are accused of violating, and then things will go from bad to worse. I urge anyone who accepts a plea agreement that includes probation to follow every rule to the letter. Even something as innocuous as leaving the county could be considered a "technical violation" of your probation and present a major problem. Below, I discuss in detail the types of VOPs and what can happen if you commit them.

Violation of Probation (VOP)

When you are on probation, you are at the mercy of your probation officer. Think of him/her as your judge, jury, and, should you violate the conditions of the probation, your executioner. They cannot kill you, of course, but they do have the power to revoke your probation. If this happens, a judge will then sign a warrant for your arrest, and you will promptly be carted off to the county jail, where you will most likely be held *without bond* until your VOP hearing. Another important thing to remember is that there is no statute of limitations for probation violations. This is true whether you live in Florida or any other state.

Just as there are different kinds of probation, there are different kinds of probation violations. As I mentioned above, a "technical violation" may be minor, but it is a violation nonetheless and can cost you a lot of time, money and heartache. Technical violations include failing to show up for an appointment with your probation officer, or not paying fines that were part of the probation agreement.

Then there are the more serious violations. For example, if you are charged with another crime while on probation, all bets are off. Remember those constitutional rights you forfeited? Well, they included your right to be judged by a jury of your peers; instead, a judge will decide whether you violated. Even worse, the burden of proof of your violation is based not on "beyond a reasonable doubt" as in most criminal cases, but the much less stringent standard of a "preponderance of the evidence". This means the prosecution has to show that it's "more than likely" that you violated. You can even be called as a witness against yourself!

If you are found guilty of violating your probation, there is a good chance that you'll be sent to prison. If not, they will most likely lengthen the probation period and/or add more conditions.

In the meantime, you may also face some serious consequences while waiting to learn your fate. The first thing to remember is that if you are accused of violating your probation, you will be held *without bond*.

Let's say, for example, that you are on probation for a crime committed in Palm Beach, then are later arrested for something else in Broward County, you will first be booked in the Broward County jail—both for the VOP and any new charges—and you will sit there for up to a week.

When they are good and ready, the Department of Corrections will arrange for a transport to the Palm Beach County Jail. When you arrive—and assuming your paperwork was not lost in transit—you will be rebooked. At that time, you will finally be allowed to contact an attorney to set the VOP hearing in front of *the original judge* that set up your probation. This is the only way to get out of jail after violating probation.

The VOP hearing is usually held before the same judge who accepted the original plea. Keep in mind that this judge will not be in any rush to see you. Remember, you have broken the trust the criminal justice system placed in you when they gave you probation. Your comfort is last on their list of priorities; in fact, it could take twenty or thirty days before the hearing is even scheduled!

Once you finally get in front of the sentencing judge, he/she will review the violation to determine whether it was a small technical violation, like leaving the county without permission, or something more serious like getting arrested on a new charge.

If it was a small technical violation, the judge may let you go with time served, or add more time to your probation. Remember, by this point, you've already spent thirty to sixty days in jail just waiting for that hearing. For more serious violations, the judge may decide to send you to jail for the remainder of your probation period. In addition, if the adjudication was withheld on the original charge, it is within his/her discretion to adjudicate it. This is why it is so important that you do not violate the terms of your probation; it can quite literally change the course of your life.

There is another program that some states, including Florida, offer for non-violent or first time offenders. It's called Pre-Trial Diversion, and it is exactly how it sounds—the program diverts the case out of the courts. And while Pre-Trial Diversion technically falls under the umbrella of probation, it has some very important differences. Those on Pre-Trial Diversion do not have to report to a Probation Officer, and their pictures are not displayed on the Department of Corrections website.

In addition, when a person enters the Pre-Trial Diversion they are not taking a plea. There are, however, some conditions placed on them; for example, the state's attorney may require them to attend classes.

Barring any mishaps (like being rearrested), the program will send the state's attorney's office a letter of successful completion of the program. He or she will then "nolle prosequi" (drop the charges), but this does not mean they have been erased from your record. However, some states, including Florida, allow you to seal and expunge your record, but like everything else in the criminal justice system, it involves a process.

I will discuss this further in the next chapter. For now, suffice it to say that this is the greatest benefit of this program: unlike probation, you can move on from Pre-Trial Diversion with a (relatively) clean slate.

Every state has slightly different laws on probation, but the basic laws are similar. If you are a disciplined person and can comply with the rules, you will be fine. Unfortunately, a lot of people refuse to follow the very simple rules of probation and find themselves being rearrested and facing some dire consequences. The important thing is to be informed of your rights and responsibilities so that you can stay out of jail and eventually move on with your life. As you will read in the next chapter, there are things you must do (including sealing and expunging) to protect and/or repair your reputation from the damages resulting from your arrest.

CHAPTER 8
Knowing Your Rights And Options After a Conviction

How to Seal or Expunge a Criminal Record

Let's face it, most of us—no matter who we are, where we're from, or what our religious beliefs are—have done something wrong at some point in our lives. It may have been something small like taking a piece of candy from the corner store, or it may be a much more serious offense, but I don't believe there is person out there who can say they have NEVER committed an illegal act. Sometimes, we have no idea we have broken the law.

In 2009, the Wall Street Journal published an op-ed by L. Gordon Crovitz entitled "You Commit Three Felonies a Day". Crovitz explores our legal system in Information Age—particularly the growing number of laws that have not caught up with technology, are vague or over-broad, or both. He also contends that the requirement of intent—a cornerstone of our criminal justice system—is disappearing. Lack of knowledge of the law has never been a defense to a crime; however, now you don't even have to intend to commit a crime in order to get in trouble. This is truly terrifying.

Take me, for example. Remember that before building the websites that led to the "sting" of my technicians and my own arrest, I asked three different attorneys whether my business strategy was illegal. All three told me that while it was "not nice", it was not a criminal offense and that, if anything, I would be sued by other locksmiths in civil court. Now, either those three attorneys all happened to be incompetent, or the law was vague. The fact that I consulted with these attorneys proves that I lacked the intent to commit a crime. However, that was irrelevant to the cops and the prosecutors. Add to this Florida's overly-broad money laundering statute, and it created a perfect storm that could have landed me in prison for twenty years.

Those of us who commit crimes fall into two categories: those who get away with it (either because they are criminal masterminds or are just plain lucky) and those who get caught, arrested and prosecuted. Whether you're "lucky" or not often depends on where you live.

Back in New York, if someone wrote a bad check to a merchant and that merchant called the police, they may give them a case number and tell them to take the "perp" to small claims court.

Here, in the police state known as South Florida, the cops would take the merchant's complaint and sometimes even go to the scene of the "crime".

We've talked quite a bit about what happens after you've been charged with a crime; it does not matter whether you are found guilty by a jury or if you take a plea. Either way, you will have a conviction on your record. If it is for a misdemeanor or a white-collar felony and it is your first offense, you will most likely be given a lighter prison sentence, or even be able to avoid jail altogether.

As I stated in an earlier chapter, many people plead guilty to crimes that they did not commit to avoid the cost and risk of a trial. However, that does not mean life will go on as usual. There are many consequences to being arrested beyond jail, especially for those who accept a plea deal. These deals are the equivalent of a guilty verdict; therefore, some people lose their jobs, especially those who work in industries requiring a professional license. Your license will be revoked or suspended, and you will be unable to earn a living.

But what many people do not know—and what I find most upsetting—is that even when the case against you has been dismissed, it can still ruin your professional (and personal) life. Let's say for example that you have been arrested for theft. And let's say that it is later discovered that another individual committed the crime. They drop the charges, arrest the real guilty party, and you are home free—sort of. While the FBI file on you now says "Case Dismissed", it does not state why it has been dismissed; it could have been anything from a lack of evidence to some other technicality. It does not let people know that you are just plain innocent, and while it won't bar licensing, it will certainly make you an unappealing choice to private employers. Even a private employer, while they won't tell you that was part of their decision—because technically, that is illegal—they will choose someone else for that job position, especially if the case was dismissed for a Violent Crime. Fortunately, some states (like Florida) will remove the entire record from your FBI arrest file. Unfortunately, other states, including New York, do not.

If you are lucky enough to live in a state like Florida that offers "Seal or Expunge", you will be able to have the case removed from your record. The main difference between the two is minor; however, if you apply to expunge rather than seal a record, the prosecuting state attorney must sign off on it (in addition to other paperwork), then the record is completely destroyed once the court order is issued. If the record is sealed, you have all the same rights as an expungement (keeping in mind that in some cases the court can order the record opened).

Whether you seal or expunge the record, the effect is exactly the same: under the law, you are within your rights to deny or fail to acknowledge the arrest or con- viction for which the record was sealed. This includes job applications, which protects your ability to earn a living. I personally recommend complete expungement if the state attorney will sign off on it. In most cases, they will, and it will take just a bit longer, but then the record is completely destroyed.

I want to be very clear, however, that not all cases are eligible to seal or expunge. The first thing to know is that whatever the case, it can only be done once in your lifetime. Once a case is either sealed or expunged, you can never apply again, even if it is in a different state. That means if you get arrested again, that second case will remain on your record. Seal and expungement are interchangeable—if you had one charged expunged, you cannot have a second charged sealed; it's one or the other, and only once. This is a great deal if you actually commit-ted the first crime; however, if you were falsely accused, then you are using your one legal seal or expunge to get rid of a charge that never should have happened in the first place.

So what is eligible? If the state you live in offers "seal or expunge" laws, you can always seal or expunge a case that was dismissed completely. After all, "dismissed" just means that the charges were dropped.

At this point, you may be thinking, *Well if it was dismissed, why would I want to seal or expunge that charge?* Well, if you're self-employed, you might not want to bother, as no government agency can ever deny a license if a case was dismissed. However, if you work for (or want to work for) a private employer, especially a large company that runs background checks, the charge will still show up on your record as arrested and dismissed. If this is the case, you are at the mercy of employers who may not be willing to take a chance on you or will deem you a criminal even if the charges were completely dismissed.

For example, let's say that, like my friend from Brooklyn, you are arrested for sexual assault. Months later, the cops find out that another person committed the crime, so they drop the charges against you, and the case is dismissed. On your FBI arrest record, it will say, "Arrested for sexual assault," and the disposition will say, "Dismissed," but this will not matter to your current or potential employer. People will always judge you for an arrest like that, and the company will not want the risk and liability of having you in the office. Chances are you will be fired, or not hired in the first place. Again, if the case is dismissed or you were found not guilty by a jury, it cannot legally be used against you. However, I assure you that in most cases, a private employer will find some other reason to fire you. That's why it is probably in your best interests to have the case expunged.

A state attorney cannot object to an expungement on a dismissal or a not guilty verdict, so if it is something major like that, by all means get that done. If, on the other hand, the charge is a minor misdemeanor like "petty theft", you might not want to waste your one and only use of this law. Remember, if you are ever arrested for a more serious crime, you will not be able to seal or expunge. Even if it's ten, twenty or thirty years later, that serious charge will be on your record and can ruin your life.

I strongly believe that if a case is dismissed or you are found "not guilty" by a jury, you should not have to use your only seal or expunge. Instead, the state should be required by law to remove the entire record at no cost to you.

In most states, the only other way you can have a case

sealed or expunged is if there is an "adjudication withheld." This means that technically you were not convicted
of the charge.

Now you might be thinking, *If that were the case, why
would I bother applying to seal or expunge at all?* Well as
I stated above, it will still show up on your record, and
people will most likely judge you for it.

It's also important to remember that there are major differences between a dismissal of charges, or a Not Guilty
verdict, and adjudication withheld on a criminal charge.
Attorneys routinely put adjudication withheld in the
same category as a not guilty verdict, but this is often not
the case at all!

Take for example, the procedure for getting a gun permit
in Florida. If you are found not guilty of a crime, there is no
problem, but if there has been an adjudication withheld,
you must wait three years to apply. This, in my opinion,
is a huge difference (and injustice). In one breath you are
being told you are not convicted, and in the next you are
being denied the chance to apply for certain licenses for
a specified period of time. It is also an issue for the legislature to decide once and for all and express that decision
clearly to the public. If a court decides an individual is not
a convicted felon, they should not be able to deny you a
license. Many people would not accept a plea if they knew
the rights that would be denied or suspended as a result.

If you think it is bad to be denied a gun license, let's take a
look at the license for a stockbroker. On the stockbroker's
application, it clearly states you *cannot even apply* if you

have been convicted of a felony—even if "adjudication was withheld"—until ten years have passed. It then goes on to say, "This shall not apply if the record has been sealed or expunged."

That's why it is so important that you research the law in your state before you take that plea deal being offered to you to make sure that the adjudication withheld will not affect your current professional license or one you may be seeking in the future. As I said above, a seal or expunge will not affect the license and is still probably a good idea, especially if it's your first offense.

Even after my experience (and several close readings of Florida laws), I still find loopholes and exceptions that I had not been aware of. On certain charges, even if "adjudication is withheld" they cannot be sealed or expunged. Some states exclude organized scheme to defraud, DUI, sexual assault, and several others. You must be proactive, do your own research, and consult a diligent, qualified attorney to be sure you are making the right decisions for yourself.

Now, if you have ever been "Adjudicated Guilty" of any crime you can NEVER, no matter if it was a felony or misdemeanor or which state it occurred, be able to seal or expunge the current or past charge.

Let's say for example that you were charged with a misdemeanor as an 18-year-old in New York, and you pled guilty (remember that New York does not offer withholds). Now, you move to Florida, and twenty years later, you are charged with grand theft. You plead guilty to this charge as well, and the prosecutor offers to "withhold adjudication". If you're thinking you can seal or expunge it at a later date, think again.

Unfortunately, there are no exceptions to this aspect of the seal or expunge law. That is why I urge you to be honest with your attorney about all your prior records before you take your plea, including where they occurred. You can then check to see whether your previous state offers withholds.

You should also note that federal law does not recognize "state law withholds". They count it as a conviction for a federal license. For example, if you plead guilty to grand theft in Florida, and the state offers you a withhold, your federal firearms license application will still be denied unless the charge has been sealed or expunged.

So what does a person do when they live in a state that does not offer seal or expunge, and perhaps does not even offer withholds? Do they have any options at all?

Anyone convicted of a felony loses their civil rights—they cannot vote anymore, and they certainly cannot own a firearm. After all, they are now a criminal, a "bad person", and according to many states, including New York, they are undeserving of a second chance.

Well, all is not lost! While arguably the seal and expunge option is the best, there are other ways to get your life in order. I know, because I have personally done it.

In 1982, while living in New York City, I pled guilty to one count of criminal mischief in the third degree—a Class

E felony—and under that state's law was not able to get a withhold or seal or expunge that record. Before I explain what it is, I must remind you that you if have been charged with a serious crime like murder, kidnapping, rape or some other violent offense, this is not for you. However, if it is a small charge, or most third-degree felonies like grand theft or any non-violent crime, you will be able to obtain almost any license you need.

So what is this great thing? It's called a Certificate of Relief of Disabilities, also known as Civil Rights Restoration, and almost every state offers it. Although, you have to be patient and willing to undertake a long process.

You need to file a form, with which I recommend you get help from an attorney, but if granted, it will restore all of your civil rights. Once you get that certificate, you can get almost any license you want (some states now require those seeking a firearm license to have the words "With the specific authority to bear arms" on the certificate). When I got mine in New York over thirty years ago, it was a blanket certificate, and it included any license. The only exception on my certificate is that I can't run for public office.

That certificate made an enormous difference in my life; I even was able to obtain a New York City gun permit, which is difficult even for those with a squeaky-clean record. Again, always check the laws of your state.

The purpose of this book is to help those who are trying to get their life back together after making a mistake. I believe everyone who makes a mistake should get a second chance. Like anything else in life, you should never give up on your legal rights; even if you fail at first and the situation looks dire, you must continue to fight. I always do.

In 1989, I fought the state of Florida and lost, but I did not give up. I appealed and was able to beat the state in the following landmark decision.

The year before, in 1988, I had applied for a Florida gun license. On the application, it clearly stated that if you had been convicted of a felony, you were disqualified. However, there was an exception to statute 790.23, which stated, "This section shall not apply to a person who has had their civil rights restored."

Well, I had a felony conviction on my record, but the state of New York had subsequently restored my civil rights. When applying for the license in Florida, I admitted to the felony, conviction, included a certified copy of my Civil rights restoration from New York, and received my license.

I thought all was well until eight months later, when I received a letter from the Division of Licensing stating that my gun license had been revoked because my civil rights had not been restored in Florida with the specific authority to bear arms.

I appealed that decision to the licensing board and lost the case. I read the law carefully and did a lot of research on it. I even checked out the federal firearms laws and found that it was the same as the states': "You cannot apply if you have a felony conviction..." However, there was an exception: "...unless you have had your civil rights restored in the state where the conviction occurred." I thought that made a lot of sense. *How could Florida restore my civil rights for a crime that had occurred in New York?* It would not have the authority to do so.

Determined to get to the bottom of this, I contacted several attorneys who all said this case was a loser. No one dared go against their "final decision."

Well, I would not give up. I hired a very young lawyer, just out of law school in fact. She told me that if I did all the work and cited the cases, she would file the brief. She figured she had nothing to lose but two hours of her time as these appeals with the Fourth District Court of Appeals are in writing and in most cases never require a court appearance. She said she would charge me only $500, and I agreed.

On December 24, 1989, she phoned me in complete shock. "I can't believe this!" she exclaimed, "We won by a per curium decision!"—which, in layman's terms, means it was unanimous.

It was a win-win for both of us. I got to keep my license, and since no one had won this type of case against the state of Florida before, it made Westlaw. This was considered a great accomplishment for an attorney just out of law school. A copy of that decision is included in the back of this book.

Chapter 9
Traffic Stops

If you have a driver's license, odds are you have been pulled over at least once for either a parking or moving violation. It's practically a rite of passage for teenagers and other new drivers, and as for the rest of us, well, who hasn't made an illegal u-turn or misjudged a yellow light? Usually, the worst part of being pulled over is getting a large ticket; however, it can be a rather scary experience. That's why it's so important to react properly during a traffic stop; it may even help you avoid a ticket.

Like most of the other topics in this book, I am speaking from personal experience. Since 1985, I have been pulled over about twelve times, yet, I have only been ticketed three times, and I have never lost a ticket in court. There are several simple things you can do to avoid a ticket, or, if you are ticketed, have it dismissed in court.

It can be jarring to see those flashing lights in your rear-view mirror, but unless there is a warrant for your arrest (or if you are doing something illegal), there is nothing to fear from a traffic stop. Let's face it, nine times out of ten, when a cop pulls you over, you've made a mistake of some kind, and you know exactly what it is. You were speeding or you ran a stop sign or you were fiddling with the radio and veered over the white line. Once in a great while, they may just be conducting a spot check to see if you have a valid license, registration and insurance, but that is a rarity. Traffic stops don't happen because the police are out to get you; however, it is a fact that tickets generate revenue for the city or town in which you live, and part of a cop's job is to bring in that money.

The first thing to remember when you get pulled over is to always keep your hands where the officer can see them. Don't make any sudden movements. An officer never knows what he or she is going to find when they make a traffic stop—it might be a perfectly-nice person, or it may be a gang member who will kill at the drop of a hat—so don't give a cop any reason to consider you a threat.

When the officer gets out of the car, roll down the window, and if the radio is on, turn it off. If it is nighttime, the same rules apply, but you should also turn on the dome light so the car is well lit for the officer. Again, the aim here is to make him feel as comfortable as possible.

When they reach the car, most police officers will ask, "Do you know why I pulled you over?"

If you know the answer (which you probably do) always reply, "Yes, officer, I might have been going over the speed limit," or, "I was not paying attention, and maybe I did not stop fully at that stop sign," or whatever it was. NEVER say that you don't know why you were pulled over unless you really don't. ALWAYS tell the officer how sorry you are and that you made a mistake. Usually you are careful, but today you were not. Most people laugh at me when I tell them how I handle my traffic stops, but it has worked for me 90% of the time. One reason for this is that I never argue with the police officer. In fact, I am always extremely polite, even if he does issue me a ticket! If you are nasty or sarcastic, the situation can quickly escalate and might even lead to an arrest. Keep in mind that the a police officer deals with criminals and other unpleasant people day in and day out, so it may not take much to make him/her angry. All a cop has to do is call for backup, and before you know it, a simple traffic stop has turned into a nightmare. Tickets can be expensive, but they are still a lot cheaper than getting arrested. Be polite, admit you were wrong, then fight the ticket in court.

Yes, even if you admit your fault, you can fight it before a judge; in fact, this is the only time to fight it, NOT with the police officer. Most people are unaware that when the police officer is writing out the ticket, they are also making notes on your behavior on the back of their copy. If you were very pleasant, he might not even show up at the court date, which means the case will most likely be dismissed. However, if you were nasty and argumentative, you can be sure the officer will be there to tell the judge all about it.

If you decide to fight the ticket and have a good driving record, always hire an attorney who specializes in traffic tickets. I can personally recommend the "Ticket Clinic"; they have represented me in several ticket cases and have been successful every time. Still, part of the reason they were able to help me is because I had followed the rules during the traffic stop.

Here's an example of how I used my good manners and common sense to avoid not one ticket, but two.

It was Labor Day weekend eight years ago, and my wife and I had gone to dinner on Sanibel Island. After a delicious meal and a few glasses of wine, we left the restaurant at about 9pm. I pulled out of the parking lot and onto a very dark road eventually coming to an intersection with a four-way flashing red light. Like many people, I have always hated four-way stop signs and flashing red lights, because no one really knows who should go when. That night was no different; I needed to make a left to get to the bridge that would take us off Sanibel Island, and after a few moments, I grew impatient and took the turn, fast. Unfortunately, I cut off an SUV in the process. As soon as I made that turn, he put up a "blue light"; it was an unmarked police vehicle! My wife was understandably very nervous; after all, I had just cut off a police vehicle after a few glasses of wine.

"Just let me handle it," I told her, but of course I was very nervous as well—so nervous in fact that when I pulled out my driver's license it slipped out of my hands and into the console.

I was reaching in to retrieve it as the officer approached my car. When I saw him coming, I immediately rolled down the window and turned on the dome light. The officer was already very angry, as anyone would've been after just getting cut off. He was also nervous as well because he saw me with my hand in the console. I immediately placed my hands on the wheel, but he had already seen me reaching somewhere.

"Sir, do you know why I pulled you over?"

"Absolutely, Officer, I was a big dummy tonight; I was not watching what I was doing, and I did not make a full stop at the four-way red light. I cut you off, and I am very sorry."

He was so taken aback by my honesty that his jaw dropped open.

"As I was approaching your vehicle, I noticed you reaching down by the console. Do you have a weapon in the car?"

"No, Officer, I don't. I was so nervous and upset about what I had done that I dropped my license in there. I was getting it ready for you so you could give me a ticket!" I was actually laughing when I told him that.

He wasn't laughing, though. He asked me to step out of the car; then he shined his flashlight in the console and saw my license. He let me bend over and get it, slowly, as he was watching. I handed it to him along with my registration and insurance card, then he told me to get back in the car and wait for him to return. As he walked back to his car to check my document, my wife turned to me and said, "You know you are going to get two or three tickets for this."

"Okay, so I get some tickets," I replied. "It happens. Let's just enjoy the rest of our night." Like I said earlier, it is only a ticket, so it's best not to make a big deal out of it.

Five minutes passed before the police officer came back

to my car, and despite what I had told my wife, I had to admit I was getting a little frightened. What if he had smelled the wine on my breath?

When the officer reappeared at my window, I noticed that he was only holding my paperwork. As long as I live, I will always remember this experience. He gave me back my stuff and thanked me for being so polite and telling him what I did. He warned me to be more careful and said, "There's a lot of traffic here, let me hold up the traffic for you so don't cut anyone else off." As he walked away, he said, "Remember, the rules are the same here as they are in Ft. Lauderdale."

And that was that—no ticket, no problem. As you see, I turned this into a good experience because I was polite, nice, and honest. To this day, my wife still doesn't understand how I got out of that!

A dashcam is also helpful in avoiding or defending against traffic tickets. People are obsessed with all the new technological gadgets, however, they usually overlook this one. A standard dashcam will record the front and back of your car, while a really good one will also record the driver's side of your car and even voices. The dashcam captures everything you do while driving and can be used in court just like any other video recording device. It is great in an accident if you were not at fault, or if you are pulled over by the police for a traffic stop. It will record not only how you were treated by the police officer, but how you responded to him or her, so obviously you shouldn't use it if you were nasty, as it will work against you in front of the judge.

A top of the line dashcam will cost about $250 to $300, but it will save you money in the long run. In fact, some insurance companies are even willing to give you a discount for having this device installed in your car.

My dashcam has saved me from at least one ticket. I'd had it in my car for about six months when I was pulled over by a police officer. When he asked me if I knew why he had pulled me over, I answered honestly that I did not. He said that he did not see me wearing my seat belt. The thing was, I had been wearing it—I had taken it off only after getting pulled over so I could reach my wallet and get my license out.

After politely explaining that I always wear a seatbelt, as it had saved my life ten years earlier when I was involved in a serious accident, I said, "I never argue with a police officer, but I want you to know I have a dashcam mounted on my windshield. Go ahead and give me a ticket, and I will bring the video to court."

The minute I said that, his demeanor completely changed. "Okay, then, I must have been wrong." He then handed my license back, told me to drive safely, and sent me on my way. So you can see, the dashcam is an excellent investment. If you know you are wrong, you don't have to use it; however, if you are right, it will prove your case.

A common misconception is that if you get a speeding ticket by radar, it is unbeatable, but this is actually far from the truth. In fact, speeding tickets by radar are among the easiest to win in court. Regardless of why you were stopped, though, remember to NEVER argue with the police officer. Save your argument for the court. Always be polite during the stop, be honest with the officer, and tell him to have a nice day. If you heed this advice, you may avoid a ticket; if you do not, you could be inviting a world of unnecessary trouble into your life.

Below, I have given you a YouTube link to one of the best traffic ticket attorneys in the country. Let him or an attorney argue your ticket in court.

https://www.youtube.com/watch?v=I83LNJgFE0Y

Now that we have covered the simple traffic stops, I will get into the much more serious implications of getting pulled over by the police.

DUI Traffic Stops

First of all, this section is not about defending drunk drivers. There is no excuse for getting behind the wheel when you're intoxicated—you can kill someone, including yourself. At the very least, you are running the risk of totaling your car and/or someone else's. Even if neither of these things happen, if a cop stops you for drunk driving, you can get arrested, pay large fines, and even go to jail. Depending on your profession, you may lose your job, and your name will be ruined.

The unfortunate truth, however, is that you do not have to be intoxicated for a police officer to arrest you for drunk driving. If you have even a small amount of alcohol in your system and get into an accident, you can be deemed completely responsible, even if the other driver actually caused it!

Many people are unaware that it can take just a few drinks to exceed the legal limit. If your blood alcohol content is over 0.08%, you are considered drunk; however, a cop could decide you are "impaired" even if your blood alcohol level is lower than that. It will be the cop's word against yours, and if you have any alcohol in your system, you can end up with a DUI on your record. But as with most things in the legal system, there are ways to stay out of trouble as long as you know your rights.

Your Vehicle

In many cases, cops must have probable cause to interfere with your liberty. When it comes to your car, that standard can be pretty low. For example, if a cop observes you speeding, driving without a seatbelt, or running a light, they have probable cause to pull you over. That's why it's so important to obey the rules of the road, especially if you've had a drink or two. Since any defect on your vehicle—a burned-out tail light, for example—also constitutes probable cause, be sure to check all lights on your vehicle every few weeks. Also be sure to check your turning signals.

Cops also look for things like loose or hanging license plates and expired inspection and registration stickers, so check those on a regular basis as well. Be aware that cops like to pull over cars with dark tinted windows, cracked windows, and loud exhausts, so either fix these things or know you risk greater scrutiny from the police.

Another law enforcement trade secret is that cops often check up on random license plates. While they're riding around, they call in the plates to a central computer. If a vehicle is registered to someone with a drunk driving conviction, you can bet they will find a reason to pull that person over.

Traffic Laws

As I said above, it's important to follow the rules of the road. But remember that driving overcautiously, such as going *under* the speed limit, is also a red flag for cops. When you see a cop, don't try too hard to prove that you're sober. Just act naturally, and wear your seatbelt. This is especially important if you're driving home late at night after leaving a bar, concert or other social event where people are known to drink. If you know less-crowded back roads, it may be wise to take those routes.

What to Do If You're Stopped

No matter how careful you are, you may find yourself being pulled over, whether it's because you made a simple error or because the light over your license plate is out. What if that night you had a couple of drinks? You know you're not impaired, but you are still justifiably nervous. Here are a few things you can do to make this easier.

Keep your registration and insurance card in a safe, easily accessible place. Also, always wait to find a safe spot to pull over, and always on the right side. As I mentioned before, keep your hands visible, roll down the window, and at night, turn the dome light on.

Here is where the advice differs from a routine traffic stop: be courteous, but admit to nothing! Do not talk about the one drink you had, because you would still be admitting to having alcohol; this can be used against you in court. All you have to give them is your license, registration and insurance. Even if he asks you point-blank whether you've been drinking, you do not have to answer.

The cop may ask you to get out of your car so he can test your physical coordination—he can ask you to walk in a straight line or recite the alphabet backwards. While it is legal for him to ask, it is also legal for you to decline. He is trying to justify what he really wants to do, which is to give you a chemical test (breathalyzer) to determine your blood alcohol content.

This is where most people find themselves in a catch-22. If you refuse to take a chemical test, there may be consequences, including the suspension of your license and criminal charges. Even lawyers are split on whether you should consent to a breathalyzer, blood or urine test. States are also divided on this issue.

From DUI.findlaw.com (as of July 2014):

Under "implied consent" laws in all states, when they apply for a driver's license, motorists give consent to field sobriety tests and chemical tests to determine impairment. Should a driver refuse to submit to testing when an officer has reasonable suspicion that the driver is under the influence, the driver risks automatic license suspension along with possible further penalties.

Consequences for breathalyzer refusal vary by state, which may explain the wide variance in statewide refusal rates, but most states impose an automatic six- or twelve-month driver's license suspension upon refusal of a BAC test. Suspensions usually increase for a refusing motorist with past DUI convictions, sometimes including jail time. License suspension following a refusal may also cause your car insurance company to cancel your policy. In many states, if the driver is found guilty of DUI, having refused the breathalyzer can result in enhanced penalties.

Here is a sample of state DUI laws with respect to breathalyzer test refusal:

California: Can result in a citation for refusing a chemical BAC test; consenting to a blood draw after initially refusing a breathalyzer exempts the suspect from a refusal charge

New York: Automatic six-month license suspension plus a possible $500 fine

Massachusetts: Six-month automatic license suspension, but refusal cannot be used to imply guilt in a DUI case; lifetime suspension for refusal after three prior DUI offenses

Ohio: Mandatory minimum six-day jail sentence or three

days in jail plus a 72-hour driver intervention program, and a fine, for those with a prior DUI conviction (20-day sentence if it's the second DUI charge in six years).

Sometimes, you do not have a say in whether you take a breathalyzer, as in certain cases, a cop can get a "roadside warrant" to test you. However, you should still watch what you say and be wary of what the officer says and does.

For example, the officer should tell you about "implied consent"—the consequences of refusing to take the test; otherwise, you may be able to get the test results thrown out of court later on.

You can also request that the officer record the stop (this is obviously unwise if you are impaired). It is within your rights to record the stop so that a judge can see that you are not in fact staggering or slurring your words. This video can be a lifesaver later on.

I know that it can be very intimidating to be stopped by a police officer, but remember that you still have rights. Although, sometimes these rights are violated in very subtle ways.

For example, if the officer insists on sticking a flashlight in your face or in your car, it may be because the flashlight is equipped with an electronic alcohol sensor. If this is the case, you have every right to tell the officer to stop. Also, just because a cop has pulled you over does not mean he can look inside your car. Absent of probable cause (or in some states, reasonable suspicion that there is a weapon or some other contraband), an officer must ask your permission. You should NEVER give this permission, even if the police officer tries to make you feel like you're acting "guilty" to refuse it.

If the cop determines that you should be tested, you usually have a choice of a breathalyzer, urine, or blood test. Contrary to popular belief, a breathalyzer test is actually an inaccurate method for testing blood alcohol content. Some states have even limited their use in court. Still, while they are being used, if your results are less than 0.08, the cops have no right to hold you. If the test results are questionable, your attorney can challenge this in court.

Chapter 10
Wrongly Convicted

Throughout this book, I have focused on people who, like me, were wrongly charged with a crime. I was wrongly charged because, if anything, my behavior constituted trademark infringement for which I could be sued in civil court. Many people are often accused of actual crimes but have been misidentified as the perpetrator. Whatever the circumstances, being wrongly charged is an ordeal that no person should have to endure.

However, as I explained in previous chapters, the person can usually get bonded out of jail unless they've been arrested for a violent crime. They can at least sleep in their own beds while they are trying to prove their case. In some cases, the charges will be dismissed or down-filed to a lesser charge that carries no prison time.

But what about those people—countless people—who have been not only wrongly charged, but wrongly convicted? They spend years or decades in prison for crimes they did not commit; some have even been put to death only to be exonerated posthumously by DNA of some other evidence.

When writing this book, I received an email that sent a

chill down my spine. The person, who obviously wanted to remain anonymous, wrote about hundreds of teachers (two-hundred each year in Broward County alone) and others who work with children who are falsely accused of child abuse or neglect. As you can imagine, their careers and lives were ruined; after all, can you think of anyone lower in our society (and rightfully so) than someone who hurts kids? Even convicts in prison hate child molesters, and they often have to be removed from the general population. Now imagine, as this person wrote in the email, being falsely accused of such a heinous offense simply because someone does not like them or wants them removed from their job. The teacher or childcare worker is guilty until they can prove they are innocent; even when the school board "police" determine that there is no probable cause, the state and the district attorney often move forward with the prosecution.

According to this email, they even have a formula—5% of cases are "guilty". While waiting for the case to go to court, many of these teachers are reassigned to menial jobs outside the classroom; this usually lasts for about a year or so. Some people of course are wrongly convicted and go to real jail after that, but even those who do not are afraid to go back to the classroom for fear that their enemies will accuse them again.

While I was a bit shocked to learn that this happens to so many teachers in Florida, I was not surprised to hear that many of those in the legal system were more concerned with building their careers than determining whether the accused were really guilty or not. And, as is the case with so many of the wrongly charged, many of these teachers accept plea bargains rather than go through the emotional and financial agony of a trial.

If you have never been in this position, you may be wondering, how is this possible in the United States? After all, our legal system has all these checks and balances in place, right? We have a Fifth Amendment right not to incriminate ourselves; hearsay can only be used under limited circumstances, and if all else fails, DNA evidence will exonerate us ... right?

If anything, defendants have too many rights; after all we are always hearing about guilty people getting off "on a technicality". So how could a truly innocent person be convicted of a crime?

First, there are the legal costs. Trials costs a lot of money—there are the attorney's fees as well as witnesses and other court costs. On paper, we as Americans do have a number of legal rights; but the truth of the matter is that it takes money to enforce them.

A good legal defense costs in the tens of thousands of dollars. It sometimes even runs into the six figures. Most people do not have this kind of money lying around, and if they cannot raise it, they may be forced to use Legal Aid or the public defender. I am not saying this to disparage these attorneys—they are often the poor person's only hope of getting legal assistance. But as talented or committed as they may be, they are also overworked and underpaid. They have so many cases, they know their clients by number more than name. Now, if you were fighting for your life in court, would you rather have a harried lawyer with stacks of files on her desk, or an attorney who has not only the legal expertise to handle your case but the time to concentrate on it?

The state and federal governments have virtually unlimited resources for expert witnesses (think of all the taxes you pay) and the other costs needed to prosecute you. Only the very wealthiest among us can afford an attorney who can go toe to toe—financially speaking—with a prosecutor. The people who cannot afford these attorneys are the ones who usually end up taking a plea bargain; even if it includes prison time.

Second, sometimes, people are convicted on circumstantial evidence. You could be at the wrong place at the wrong time, and witnesses can make a mistake in identifying you. If you are lucky, there may be DNA evidence to exonerate you; however, not every case involves DNA.

As bleak as this picture sounds, there are some top-tier attorneys who dedicate their time and resources to helping the innocent. In 1992, Barry C. Scheck and Peter J. Neufeld founded the Innocence Project, a nonprofit legal clinic affiliated with the Benjamin N. Cardozo School of Law in New York City. It has since grown into a network of clinics across the U.S. The attorneys at the Innocence Project review convictions, and when convinced of the person's innocence, petition the court for DNA testing. With their help, more than two hundred people have been freed from prisons based on DNA, including seventeen who were awaiting execution on death row. The Innocence Project also advocates for legal reforms that will prevent others from being wrongfully convicted.

On the next few pages, I will illustrate some of the cases where the Innocence Project has helped people and should be commended for everything they have done. Many thanks to all attorneys out there who do this pro bono work to help innocent people.

James Bain

On March 4, 1974, a nine-year-old boy was abducted from his home when a man climbed through his bedroom window. The assailant took the victim to a field near his house, where he raped him. He then released the victim, who showed up at his house wearing only his underwear and a t-shirt. The police were called to the scene, and they took the underwear, which they then sent to the FBI for serological testing (remember that there was no DNA testing back then). Serological testing identifies fluids identified at a crime scene (for example, if blood is found at the scene, this type of testing will help scientists deter-mine whether it is human or animal). It is still used today, but it is not as precise as DNA testing.

When the victim described his attacker, his uncle told the cops that it sounded like James Bain, who had attended the high school at which the uncle had been a principal. When the victim agreed that it was Bain, the cops went to Bain's house.

By the time it was midnight; Bain claimed to have been there with his sister since around 10:30 when he returned home after hanging out with his friends. He denied having anything to do with the crime, and although he had an alibi for the entire evening, he was arrested.

The trial centered mostly on the FBI's serology testing of the victim's underwear as well as his identification of Bain. The FBI analyst had testified that per the serology testing, the semen sample on the victim's underwear was blood group B, and since Bain's underwear was group AB (with a weak A), he could not be excluded as the attacker. The defense's expert witness disputed this, claiming that Bain had a strong A and therefore could not be the source of the semen.

The defense also stated that the victim had only identified Bain as his attacker after his uncle had suggested that it might be him. Until that point, the victim had given the cops a description of his assailant that included very prominent sideburns; he also said the attacker had referred to himself as "Jimmy".

When the officers took the victim to the station, they showed him pictures of five or six men. Bain's photo was included, but only one other man had the kind of prominent sideburns the boy had mentioned. This was improper, as it automatically eliminated the men with no sideburns and made it more likely for him to choose Bain. It was also revealed at trial that the cops suggested that he choose Bain's photo, rather than asking him if he saw his assailant in the photo lineup.

Due to the weight given the serology testing and the victim's identification, James Bain was convicted for kidnapping and rape. During his imprisonment, he attempted five times to get DNA testing. When an appeals courts overturned the fifth denial, the Innocent Project of Florida stepped in. The semen sample was sent to a private laboratory for DNA testing, the results of which excluded Bain as the rapist. On December 17, 2009, after serving thirty-five years for a crime he did not commit, James Bain was freed from prison. To date, this is the longest sentence served by someone later exonerated by DNA. The real rapist has never been found.

Larry Bostic

It was four a.m. on October 12, 1988. A thirty-year-old woman from Ft. Lauderdale had gone out to use a pay phone. She was on her way home when she was attacked by an African American man. He forced her at knifepoint behind a bar, ordered her to take off her clothes, then raped her. Before leaving, he took the seventy-five dollars she was carrying.

At the police station, the woman identified Bostic as her rapist from a photo lineup. Bostic was arrested and charged with sexual battery and robbery, to which he pled guilty in exchange for a sentence of eight years to be followed by five years of probation.

As part of Bostic's plea deal, he was released on probation after serving more than three years. Nine months later, however, he was arrested for violating his probation and sentenced to another seventeen years!

During the appeals process, he claimed he had pled guilty only because the prosecutor and his public defender convinced him that he would likely spend the rest of his life in prison. Furthermore, the lawyer handling Bostic's appeal stated that in 2007 the victim denied ever seeing her attacker, but had probably recognized Bostic after seeing him around the neighborhood.

In 2005, Bostic filed a handwritten motion requesting DNA testing on the victim's underwear and a rape kit collected after the crime. This is why plea deals can be so dangerous.

There was actually a law in place denying DNA testing when such a deal was in place! But in 2006, the Innocence Project of Florida fought for and won the right for those who had pled out to get DNA testing. Bostic filed again, and in June 2007, prosecutors finally agreed to allow the testing. The result: the sperm cells in the rape kits did not match Bostic. At that point, the prosecution agreed that the charges should be dismissed and conviction vacated.

On September 21, 2007, at age fifty-one and after spending eighteen years in prison, Larry Bostic was finally released and his name cleared.

William Dillon

On the morning of August 17, 1981, the body of a man was found in a wooden area near Canova Beach. The victim's name was James Dvorak, and he had been beaten to death in an area known to be a homosexual meeting place.

A few days later, William Dillon was at Canova Beach when he was approached by police. They had been questioning random people about Dvorak's murder. Dillon knew where the crime had taken place—he claimed this was because he had read about it and then saw the yellow police tape by the woods. The cops however became suspicious, brought him in for questioning, and eventually arrested him for the crime.

The prosecution was centered on the testimony of four key witnesses. The key physical evidence was a yellow t-shirt. One of the witnesses was a woman with whom Dillon had a sexual relationship. She claimed to have seen him at the scene of the murder but had not seen the crime. She claimed that Dillon was wearing the yellow t-shirt that night. She would later recant her entire testimony, saying she had been threatened by law enforcement and prosecutors with twenty-five years in jail. She admitted to lying about several details including their whereabouts on the night of the murder.

The state also called as a witness a supposed expert in scent tracking, who claimed that his dog had linked Dillon to the crime and the yellow t-shirt. His claims were disproven by others in the scent tracking field, and he was exposed as a fraud in the media.

The state's third witness, who claimed that Dillon had confessed and reenacted the murder, did so in exchange for the state dropping the charges in his rape trial. Clearly, he had a motive to lie about Dillon!

The fourth witness, who claimed to have picked up a sweaty, bloody hitchhiker on the night of the murder, may have had good intentions. He identified Dillon; however, the witness was legally blind in one eye, and his description did not hit the mark. Still, the prosecution put him on the stand.

In 2007, the Florida Innocence project won a motion for DNA testing. The DNA proved that the sweat on the bloody yellow t-shirt did not come from Dillon but from some unknown person.

On November 14, 2008, after spending more than twenty-seven years in prison for a crime he didn't commit, Dillon's conviction was vacated, and he was set free.

As you can see, despite our legal rights, there can be a perfect storm of circumstances that lead to a wrongful arrest and conviction. Below are some YouTube video links to watch. You might find them helpful. I included a link for the innocence project. Thank them for the great work they have done.

James Bain

http://www.youtube.com/watch?v=ILt7ukHHxL0

http://www.youtube.com/watch?v=indhkHcfJyM

William Dillon

http://www.youtube.com/watch?v=ikoiP9636Bo

http://www.youtube.com/watch?v=sTVn72fxYG4

The Innocence Project Founders

http://www.youtube.com/watch?v=wiyZe_
LgIOc&list=PLF1EDD9AC2EAC6389

http://www.innocenceproject.org/

I sincerely hope these stories have awakened you to an enormous problem in this country. These are real people, just like you and I, whose lives were destroyed by faulty evidence, misidentification, erroneous conclusions by witnesses, and overstepping by the police.

There is a saying—"It is better that ten guilty escape than one innocent suffer." This was stated by 18th century English jurist William Blackstone in his best-known work, *Commentaries on the Laws of England.* This principal is theoretically one of the pillars of our own legal system, but as the above cases illustrate, the innocent suffer all too often.

In Chapter 13, I will discuss the outcomes of my case, as well as those against the other two wrongly-charged locksmiths, Peter and Josh. The state of Florida spent a ton of money on these three cases and forced the defendants to do the same. But whereas the state had plenty of taxpayer money to do so, it placed an undo financial hardship on the defendants. The state knew all along that this was a civil matter, yet they pursued it as if it were the crime of the century. I made page one of the Sun-Sentinel on August 23, 2013! All this money and eight months of our lives for something that could have been dealt with—if at all—through a civil lawsuit. Why did this happen? Well, let's just say that, in a nutshell, we pissed off the wrong cop.

CHAPTER 11
Criminal Sentencing
In Florida

In the event that you are convicted at trial (or have pled guilty or no contest), the next step would be for the judge to impose punishment. I cannot speak for the laws of other states; however, I can tell you that the sentencing guidelines in Florida can be convoluted and difficult to navigate. That's why you must speak with a competent attorney before making any decisions about a plea bargain.

Before handing down your sentence, the judge may order the Florida Department of Corrections to put together a Pre-Sentence Investigation Report (PSIR). This report will contain information about the circumstances of the crime, as well as your family background, education, prior criminal history, employment, health, lifestyle, and reputation in the community. It may even include information about your personality or "general attitude".

The judge will usually postpone sentencing until he or she has received and reviewed the PSIR. Your defense attorney will also get a copy of the report (and will review it with you) as he or she prepares for the sentencing hearing. Part of this preparation includes engaging doctors or other experts to evaluate you and prepare their own sentencing report, which will have recommendations for the judge.

It is the right of those convicted of a crime to have their lawyer make a presentation at the sentencing hearing; the defendant also has the right to speak in his or her own defense. Friends and family of the defendant often speak at sentencing hearings too, presenting a different side of the person to the court and arguing for leniency.

After the judge has reviewed the PSIR and heard the statements at the hearing, he or she will inform the defendant of the finding of guilt and impose punishment per Florida's sentencing guidelines.

Depending on the crime and the circumstances, the judge may suspend the sentence, give the defendant probation, or sentence him or her to jail for the maximum amount of time allowed by law. In certain cases, the judge will order the defendant to pay restitution to the victim(s).

If the defense attorney is a public defender, the defendant may have to pay his or her legal fees as well as court costs. It may surprise you to learn that the public defender is not free unless you are acquitted. If you are found guilty, you will probably have to pay the "reasonable value" of the services the attorney provided.

Criminal sentences in Florida are determined by the Florida Criminal Punishment Code. It was mostly recently amended in 1998. However, those guidelines apply only to felonies committed on or after October 1, 1998. If you committed the offense any time before that date, you will be sentenced according to one of the previous versions of the laws, whether it's 1983, 1994 or 1995.

Prison terms in Florida are calculated according to a scoring system, which is broken down into several elements, each assigned a particular numerical value. These numbers are recorded onto a score sheet, then tallied up and fed into a formula. Your final score correlates to a length of time served in prison that is unique to your circumstances. The scoresheet must include all offenses that are currently before the court for sentencing. In addition, a different scoresheet must be filled out for crimes committed under previous sentencing guidelines. For example, if you committed a murder in December of 1998 but were not caught, tried and convicted until 2010, you would still be sentenced under the 1998 guidelines.

The responsibility for preparing each scoresheet falls to the office of the state attorney, who then distributes copies to the department of corrections, the defense attorney so he/she can check it for any inaccuracies, and the sentencing judge so he or she can review it before passing a sentence. A defense attorney can never be forced to fill out a scoresheet, as this would violate the attorney-client relationship.

The intent of the scoresheet is to cover every angle of the case. Literally every criminal offense in Florida has been assigned a value by the state legislature—whether it's a violent crime or a white-collar scheme. The more serious the crime, the higher the number. So, after some general information such as your race, gender, birthday and the date of the offense, the state attorney will enter your primary offense.

Let's say you've been convicted of robbery under Florida Statute 812.13, the state's attorney's office would add the corresponding number to your scoresheet.

Next comes any additional offenses you committed. Additional offenses are assigned less points than they would be as a primary offense. For example, the cops are called to your home on a domestic violence charge. They arrive to find that you have indeed struck your wife, and they place you under arrest. If they see drugs or drug paraphernalia on the coffee table, possession of that would be added to your scoresheet as an additional offense and assigned a smaller number than if it had been your primary offense.

A value is also assigned to any injuries your victims sustained due to your actions, again, with higher numbers for more severe injuries. For example, if you caused a person's death, 120 points are added to your sheet; if you have severely injured them, the number is 40. Sexual offenses are also distinguished and numbered according to severity, with rape carrying a higher number than inappropriate touching. Whatever the crime, each victim's injuries are calculated separately—if you caused the deaths of two people, 240 points would be added to your scoresheet and therefore calculated into your sentence.

Once the primary and additional offenses and victim's injuries have been determined, the state's attorney will then assess your legal status. This encompasses things like whether you have failed to appear for a court date, escaped from custody or were fleeing the jurisdiction; it also includes those who are incarcerated or out on pretrial release. The state will also take into account whether you have a supersedeas or "appeals" bond. This is a type of surety bond that's issued to a person who has lost their case and is appealing the decision. It postpones the judgment from being enforced until the outcome of the appeal. Legal status issues will add four points to your sentencing scorecard.

Community sanction violations also affect the calculation of your sentence. Similar to legal status, these violations involve things like probation and community control; however, they are considered more severe. Community sanction violations can add anywhere from 6, 12 or 24 points to your scorecard.

If your criminal activity involved a firearm, this will also significantly affect your scorecard—adding anywhere from 18 to 25 points. If you have prior serious felonies on your record, this can add a whopping 30 points.

Finally, your scorecard is subject to Enhancements. These are circumstances of the crime that act as multipliers, which are added after your score has been calculated. For example, the theft of a motor vehicle during your crime will multiply your score by 1.5—this is a huge deal. Let's say your robbery score is 40; if in the course of that crime you also stole a motor vehicle, those 40 points will be multiplied by 1.5, for a grand total of 60!

Once all these factors have been added in, the final number is then plugged into the following formula to arrive at the lowest possible sentence:

Number of points minus 78, then multiplied by 0.75.

At this point, your case will fall into one of two categories. If your total number of sentence points is less than 44, there is no minimum sentence. This means it is completely up to the judge; he or she can sentence you to probation, prison, or a combination of the two. If you're number is over 44, however, there is a mandatory minimum that the judge must adhere to when passing sentence.

Most of the time, your scorecard determines your prison sentence; however, there are exceptions. Certain crimes carry minimum sentences that will take precedence over your score. For example, trafficking in cocaine—even a small amount—carries a minimum of three years in prison, even if your scorecard would call for a lesser sentence.

However, under certain circumstances, it is still within the judge's discretion to lower the sentence even if it carries a mandatory minimum. For example, the judge can lower the sentence if the defendant is under the age of twenty-one even if he/she is being tried as an adult and even if there is a mandatory sentence. Another example is the "downward departure"—this is something that every defendant who "scores prison" should know about.

As we saw earlier, Florida's sentencing structure has mandatory minimums for certain crimes, and it relies on the scoring system to arrive at that sentence for each defendant. In most cases, a judge is not allowed to sentence someone below that minimum; however, under Florida Statute 921.0026(2), there are certain mitigating circumstances under which the judge can "depart" from mandatory sentences and give the defendant less prison time. An appellate court can review whether the judge was justified in granting the downward departure, but it has no say over the extent of that departure.

If you have a halfway-decent lawyer, he or she will try to make a deal with the prosecutor regarding your sentence—usually as a result of a plea bargain. However, if your lawyer was unable to do this, you can ask the sentencing judge for a downward departure.

In considering your request, the judge has to answer two questions: the first is whether he/she "can depart", which is really just a fancy way of asking whether you are eligible for a lesser sentence. The other question is whether a downward departure will result in the "best and most appropriate sentence". This means striking a balance between what is fair to the defendant and meting out an adequate punishment given the particular set of circumstances. Per the statute, the following are considered such mitigating circumstances that make a defendant eligible for a downward departure. They apply to any felony committed on or after October 1, 1998, except capital crimes.

- There is a legitimate, uncoerced plea bargain in place. This is the most common reason a downward departure is granted—because the state supports it. In very rare cases, the judge will give you even less of a sentence than what was agreed upon in the plea bargain, but don't count on it.

- You were merely an accomplice to the offense and had a relatively small role in the crime.

- At the time of the crime, your capacity to appreciate the criminal nature of the conduct or to conform that conduct to the requirements of law was substantially impaired.

- You have a mental disorder or physical disability that requires special treatment for and you are willing to undergo that treatment (this does not apply to substance abuse or addiction for offenses committed after July 1, 1997). Judges are split on this one—you might get one who is sympathetic to your condition or one who wants to throw the book at you anyway. You might have to show that you will not be able to get adequate treatment if you're incarcerated. If you also have a substance abuse problem, you'll have to prove that you already had the mental illness when you started using drugs or alcohol.

- It is more important for you to pay restitution to the victim than to be in prison. Clearly this applies primarily to white-collar crimes. The judge will take a look at how much you owe and how much you will be able to pay if released. He/she will also take a look at the urgency with which the victim needs to be repaid.

- The victim either started or was a willing partici-pant in the incident.

- You committed the crime while under extreme duress or under the domination of another person. Essentially, someone else forced you to commit the crime by threatening, blackmailing, or otherwise controlling you.

- The victim was already compensated before you were caught.

- You have worked with the state to help them solve this crime or any other crime.

- The criminal behavior was an isolated insolent, and you have shown remorse. In this case, the crime must also have been committed in an unsophisticated manner, therefore demonstrating that you're not a "pro".

- When you committed the crime you were too young to appreciate the consequences of it.

- You're being sentenced as a youthful offender. This means you must be under twenty-one at the time of sentencing. You can only take advantage of this once, and never for a felony that is eligible for the death penalty or life sentence. If the judge agrees, he/she may give a withhold adjudication or may incarcerate you for no more than six years. If the judge gives you imprisonment followed by probation, the combined sentences cannot be more than six years.

- You must have committed a nonviolent felony as defined by Florida Statute 948.08(6), and your Criminal Punishment Code scoresheet total sentence points must be 60 or fewer. The court must also determine that you are willing to participate in a post-adjudicative treatment-based drug court program and that you are qualified to participate in the program as part of your sentence. Please note that you will not otherwise be eligible for a downward departure for being drunk or high during the time of the crime, or if you have a substance abuse issue.

- During the commission of the crime, you were making a good faith attempt to help someone who had overdosed on drugs.

Other Consequences of a Criminal Conviction

While going to jail is obviously the most terrifying part of being convicted, there are other very troubling consequences that can be extremely damaging to personal and professional lives. Having a criminal record can make it difficult to find or keep a job (especially in a state like Florida, where criminal records are public), secure housing or get financial aid for school. This is true whether you go to prison or not. In addition to state benefits, convicted felons also lose some federal rights and responsibilities, such as the right to vote, serve on a jury or in the military, hold public office, or own or possess a firearm. Also, felons in Florida have to submit a sample of their DNA, which will be included in the state database.

In most cases, a convicted felon can apply to have his civil rights restored through the clemency process after completing the sentence.

Chapter 12
It Isn't Over Till It's Over

The Appeals Process

Let's say that after being wrongly charged for a crime or sued in civil court, you followed the advice in this book—you've hired a competent attorney, you've also done your own research so that you can assist with your own case. You're devastated when even after fighting the good fight, you are found guilty of the crime and liable for huge sums of money. What now? All is not lost—you may still have a chance to reverse the court's decision through an appeal.

Like every state, Florida has its own processes and procedures for appealing civil and criminal cases; while it might be tempting to represent yourself at your appeal (especially after spending all that money on legal fees at trial), it's extremely important that you find an experienced appellate attorney so you have the best chance to win your appeal.

First, though, you have to get the appeal. Contrary to what you see on TV, most appeals are not automatic. The appellate court will first review the entire record of your trial, including pleadings, pretrial motions, the trial transcript, exhibits, etc.; then it will determine whether: 1) an error was made at trial, and 2) except for that error, the outcome of the trial would have been different (in your favor).

But how does the appellate court determine whether there was an error serious enough to affect the court's decision? Anyone who's watched a courtroom drama on television has seen a lawyer indignantly rise up out of his or her seat and shout, "Objection, Your Honor!" Usually, the lawyer then states the reason for the objection. For example, the witness is giving hearsay testimony, the opposing counsel is leading the witness, asking the question in such a way as to solicit a particular answer, or the question pertains to information not relevant to the case. The judge then makes a quick decision, and the camera pans in toward the angry face of the lawyer the judge ruled against.

On the other hand, if you've seen *My Cousin Vinny*, one of the complaints was that Vinny was too inexperienced to know when to object and for what reason. Of course, once he studied the rules of evidence, he was able to more effectively argue for his clients and eventually get them acquitted.

Well, it might be funny in the movies, but it's not so funny if your real-life lawyer lets these things slip under the radar. What you may not know is that the attorney does only object in order to get a ruling at trial, he/she is also objecting to "preserve" the issue for appeal. This means the objection—and, hopefully, the reason for it—will become part of the trial record and can be reexamined later to see whether there are grounds for appeal. If the lawyer did not object to something, he or she is seen as having "waived" the issue, and it therefore becomes irrelevant for the purposes of getting or winning an appeal.

Even if the court grants you an appeal, that doesn't mean it's going to be easy to win. The standards of review for appeals, whether criminal or civil, are very different from the burden of proof at trial. In other words, the appellate court does not look at the facts from scratch as the trial court had done. Instead, it reviews the facts of the trial— and usually, the trial court's decision—with a great deal of deference. The presumption is that the trial court was competent and that it had the best opportunity to assess the facts at hand and make a sound legal decision.

As with every area of the law, much of the rules around appeals are based on precedent. For example, in the 1976 Florida case, Shaw v. Shaw, the appellate court stated, "It is not the function of the appellate court to substitute its judgment for that of the trial court through re-evaluation of the testimony and evidence from the record on appeal before it." Shaw v. Shaw, 334 So.2d 13, 16 (Fla. 1976). Basically, this means that the trial court's decision will stand unless the appellate finds that the facts of the case are just plain wrong (e.g., if the evidence does not support the defendant being at the scene of the crime) or that there was a mistake in law (e.g., if the judge included evidence that should not have been included or vice versa). Of course, the appellate court will also overturn the decision if they find an "abuse of discretion" by the lower court. This basically means the judge used unsound judgment when making his/her decision.

Sometimes, however, the appellate court will use a "de novo" standard to review. This is your best chance of winning your appeal. The term de novo means "anew"; the appellate court will examine the facts in the original trial record but apply the law and makes its own evidentiary rulings, rather than relying on those of the lower court.

Procedure for Filing an Appeal

First, you have to wait for there to be a "final judgment" entered in the case. In other words, you cannot say you want to appeal because you don't like the way the trial is going. You have to wait for the end of the trial; otherwise, the already overloaded court system would be an even bigger mess.

The Notice of Appeal gets the ball rolling—this is a simple document announcing your decision to appeal the trial court's decision. Once the final judgment has been entered, you have 30 days to file the Notice of Appeal; if you do not, the appellate court will not have the jurisdiction to hear your appeal, and it will be dismissed.

After filing the Notice of Appeal, you become the "appellant", and the opposing party (who wants the appellate court to uphold the trial court's decision) is known as the "appellee". The appellee can also file a cross-appeal if he or she chooses, but they must do so within ten days of the Notice of Appeal.

After the Notice of Appeal is filed, the appellant has ten days to file what's called the "directions to the clerk" and "designations" to the court reporter. This is commonly referred to as "pulling together the records." Basically, you are letting the clerk from the lower court know that you want to be included in the record being sent to the appellate court.

The court clerk has 50 days from the date of the Notice of Appeal to submit the trial record to the appellate court for review.

In the meantime, your attorney should be hard at work on the first appellate brief. The appellant's first brief needs to be submitted within 70 days of the Notice of Appeal being filed. This is where the lawyer's objections at trial come into play. In the initial brief, your appellate attorney should argue each objection preserved at trial, as each may turn out to be grounds to overturn the trial court's decision (e.g., if the judge overruled your lawyer's objection to prejudicial testimony, your appellate attorney can argue that the judge was wrong and that his/her decision changed the outcome of the case.) The court is not going to hear arguments or admit evidence on matters that were not heard or admitted by the original trial court.

There is also a limit to how long these briefs can be—the appellant's initial brief cannot be more than fifty pages; the same goes for the appellee's answering brief. The appellant's replying brief can only be fifteen pages. Briefs longer than this will not be considered by the court.

Once the briefs have been filed, the clerk will schedule

a date for oral arguments before a three-judge tribunal (once in a while, the appellate court will make a decision based solely on the briefs, but this is not the norm). Unlike the first trial, there are strict limits on how long the oral arguments can be—sometimes the lawyers are actually timed! That's why it's so important to hire an experienced appellate attorney, as he or she will be used to making arguments under such time constraints.

Criminal Appeals

The procedure for criminal cases is similar to that of civil matters. Criminal defendants can appeal a guilty verdict at trial, as well as an adjudication withheld. They can even appeal orders granting, modifying or revoking probation. Obviously, they can appeal an illegal sentence. Many criminal defendants base their appeals on ineffective assistance of counsel; in fact, it has become a sort of "catch-all" claim.

People sentenced to death get an automatic appeal whether they want one or not. In fact, in July 2014, the Florida Supreme Court held that a defense lawyer cannot withdraw from a case because his/her client wants the death penalty to stand.

Convicted murderer James Robertson had been sentenced to death and did not wish to contest it. When his attorney, citing his responsibility to advocate for his client's wishes, attempted to withdraw, the court would not allow him to do so, stating that it would be tantamount to helping

Robertson commit "state-assisted suicide." While it is admirable that the state is interested in making sure an innocent person is not put to death, it should have more consideration when it comes to letting innocent people rot in prison!

There are only very limited circumstances under which you can appeal after pleading guilty or nolo contendere ("no contest"). Surprisingly, you can negotiate the right to appeal as part of the plea; however, it has to have been specifically preserved in the agreement, around a specific point of law (e.g., your attorney preserves the right to appeal based on sentencing error or an involuntary plea.) You can also appeal a guilty or no contest plea based on the argument that the trial court did not have subject matter jurisdiction, or that the state violated a plea agreement.

If you're appealing a case in Florida, you'll most likely go before the District Court of Appeals. There are five District Courts of Appeal in the state: the First District is in Tallahassee, the Second District is in Lakeland, the Third District is in Miami, the Fourth District is in West Palm Beach, and the Fifth District is in Daytona Beach. These courts will hear any case that was originally adjudicated in the Circuit Courts, such as a Family Law case; a case involving probate and guardianship; or any civil case that involves more than $15,000. It also includes appeals of final decisions from an administrative agency. The District Court of Appeals also hears criminal cases such as felonies or cases involving juvenile delinquency.

If you lose your appeal to the District Court of Appeals, you can then ask the Florida Supreme Court to hear the case. This is why the appeals process can take so many years. While there are some circumstances under which the losing party always has the right to appeal to the Florida Supreme Court, for the most part, it's in the Court's sole discretion as to whether or not it reviews a case. You will just have to wait for the court's answer and hope they find your case worthy of their time.

If you're involved in a federal case, your trial was most likely held in one the United States district courts. To appeal such a decision, you'll take your case to a Federal Circuit Court of Appeals. There are thirteen 13 U.S. Courts of Appeals, usually located in major cities across the country. Florida, along with Georgia and Alabama, are located in the Eleventh Circuit, with the court itself located in Atlanta.

If you lose your case before a U.S. Court of Appeals (and in certain cases before a state appellate court), the next and final step is to file a Petition for Writ of Certiorari with the U.S. Supreme Court (SCOTUS). Not surprisingly, it is not easy to get your case before the SCOTUS, as it only hears cases that have significance far beyond the particular parties, i.e., cases in which federal courts disagreed about a federal issue (these cases are called "circuit splits"). The court will also consider issues that are very important to our society—cases involving the interpretation of the Constitution, or those in which a lower court found a federal statute unconstitutional.

There are a few federal statutes that allow for direct appeal from U.S. district courts to the Supreme Court, but most of the time, the court has complete discretion as to what cases it hears and what it rejects.

All told, the Supreme Court hears less than 5% of the cases it is asked to review each year; however, its cases are among the most important in American jurisprudence and have significantly affected our society. A few examples include, Roe v. Wade, which legalized abortion, Brown v. Board of Education, which declared racial segregation unconstitutional, and Bush v. Gore, which determined the outcome of the 2000 presidential election.

Supersedeas Bonds

As you can see, the appeals process can be an agonizingly slow one, which brings up the question: what do you do while waiting to see if your appeal has been successful? Some criminal defendants can remain free (post-trial release) during the appeals process, while others (usually more violent criminals) must appeal their conviction from a prison cell. What about if you have lost a civil case and the court has ordered you to pay damages (and probably attorney's fees) to the plaintiff? Do you have to pay while appealing your case? Fortunately, there are other options such as a supersedeas bond.

Let's say, for example, that instead of being wrongly charged with a crime, I was sued in civil court by one of the locksmith companies for trademark infringement.

Now, let's say that they win the case, and a judgment is entered against me. I feel that I did not infringe on their trademark and promptly appeal the ruling. A supersedeas bond will "stay" the judgment, which means the court will wait until the outcome of the appeal arrives before enforcing it. This would protect all parties. It would stop the court from putting a lien on my property, and it would protect the other party in the event that I was appealing just to delay payment.

Appeals take time, and there is always the chance that the losing party will no longer have the means to pay by the time it is over. Essentially, this bond is providing good faith that the losing party is good for the money and intends to pay.

In some criminal cases, the defendant, after losing at trial, can ask for post-trial release pending appeal. If the court approves, he or she will have to post bond to ensure they do not flee the jurisdiction. Either way, these bonds are typically underwritten by a surety or insurance company, which, like a bail bondsman, takes a fee for putting up the money.

It Ain't Over Till It's Over

As you have probably gathered by now, the appeals process (like everything else having to do with the criminal justice system) can be long-drawn out. Some people even serve out entire prison sentences while awaiting the final decision! The important thing, though, is to not give up.

I know how terrifying it is to be at the mercy of an unfair system, but if you have been convicted of a crime you did not commit, or have (unfairly) lost a civil suit, you must keep fighting to get those decisions overturned. Hire the best appellate lawyer you can afford, and make sure they follow the appeals process to the letter. It may just save you years of your life—not to mention thousands of dollars.

CHAPTER 13
Conclusion

My primary goal in writing this book was to educate and support those who have been wrongly charged with a crime. As you've seen here, this happens much more than the average person realizes, and unlike the criminal law TV shows so many of us are fond of watching, the nightmare is not over in sixty minutes. Instead, it can rob you of months or years of your life—sometimes even your life itself! Even if you are found innocent of the crime, your reputation, and oftentimes your ability to earn a living, can be destroyed beyond repair. While my story is not as tragic as some of those I've discussed, it did rob me of a lot of time, a lot of money, and a lot of peace of mind.

By now, you must be wondering what happened to me and the other locksmiths in the case. Remember that this all started when the Palm Beach county's State Attorney's office and the town of Palm Beach took a civil matter—namely, locksmith companies fighting over trademarks—and turned it into a criminal witch hunt, spending an exorbitant amount of taxpayer's money and God knows how many man-hours in the process. For my own protection, I am choosing not to disclose the dollar amount. I'll just tell you that the investigation lasted from

147

December 2012 through August 2013 and leave you to speculate. Suffice it to say, they've spent less time and money prosecuting murderers.

At the conclusion of the investigation, the town of Palm Beach was so proud of itself that they gave an award to "Officer Nick," the lead detective on the case. The award was presented with much fanfare and even posted on the Internet.

It did not stop there; on April 23, 2014, they had an award ceremony at the Embassy Suites in West Palm Beach, Florida. Detective Nick was awarded a Law Enforcement commendation at a luncheon by the Palm Beach Chapter of American Revolution. They nicknamed him "Honey Badger". If he had caught a murderer, maybe then might he have deserved this award!

When I read about the award, along with a laundry list of justifications for the expense to taxpayers, I couldn't help but laugh. They could list whatever they wanted; I knew of dozens of businesses that had names similar to larger companies. I had also heard of companies stealing each other's technology for smartphones and computers. However, I'd never once heard of the police getting involved. Instead, they duked it out in civil court, fighting over the right to the name, trademark or technology—and at the end of the case, one party had to cease using it and/ or write a check to the other to cover lost revenue. No one was hauled off in cuffs and charged with organized scheme to defraud and money laundering. No one was threatened with a twenty-year prison sentence.

The first part of the award congratulated the police officer because he "uncovered fraudulent websites to redirect customers."

As I explained earlier in the book, these websites were not fraudulent but legitimately offered locksmith services. People who called the number got a real locksmith who actually showed up at their homes and businesses to change the lock, then charged a fair price for services rendered. The only "victims" in this case were the three locksmiths arrested for using a company name similar to the one that does locksmithing for the Town of Palm Beach. In all the arrest affidavits, it was always stated "Similar Name," so, beware, everyone, because apparently this is now a crime in Palm Beach, Florida! Remember that it is the cops' job to enforce the law, not to reinterpret it or to create new laws—that is the job of the legislature.

It was also stated on the detective's award that he found forty websites. Well, I would love for him to show them to me. There were a total of nine or ten legally registered websites. Moreover, all of our "similar" websites contained a disclaimer at the bottom of the page stating that we were not the other company, and many of our websites even contained a link to the other company. Now, was this disclaimer smaller than the rest of the print? Sure it was, just like 99.9% of all disclaimers out there.

The second part of the award stated that the cop "stopped calls placed by unsuspecting residences and businesses that would result in individuals with unknown qualifications and motives coming to their residences or place of business."

This was another sticking point with me. As I stated earlier, there is no licensing requirement for locksmiths in the state of Florida, so what qualifications could one present? There was once a bill proposed in the state legislature that would have regulated how locksmiths operate, including certain minimum skills they must have. It also stated how a locksmith can advertise his business, and it clearly articulated penalties for unfair and deceptive trade practices. However, the bill died in the Appropriations committee on April 30, 2010, which means that the state of Florida has no measure of any kind with regard to a locksmith's qualifications. It is therefore patently unfair to single us out for having "unknown qualifications" when ALL locksmiths in Florida have unknown qualifications because the state has never set them! Perhaps we were an easy target because we were mobile locksmiths rather than having paid for a costly storefront that may have lent us some credibility. How does this affect our ability to service the public?

The phrase "unknown motives" is equally vague. In fact, our motives were quite clear—perform the job to the customers' satisfaction (which we did) and collect an honest paycheck. None of our customers reported a burglary or anything of the sort after our locksmiths were at their homes and businesses.

Even more reprehensible is that they prosecuted us for actions that the legislature failed to criminalize. If you come down a road and there is no stop sign, can the police issue a ticket for passing a stop sign? The answer is no, of course, but that does not mean you shouldn't exercise due care. That is exactly what we did when we included our disclaimer on our sites. What's more, the alleged complaints on record were only few and far between, and they were sought out by the detective.

In April of 2013, I received a surprising call from a former customer. When the woman asked me whether she should change her locks again, I had no idea what she was talking about. As she went on, I realized she thought she was reaching the other company—the one the locksmith I had was allegedly imitating. I also realized she had been contacted by the detective on the case, who was seeking out my "victims".

Curious as to where this was going, I played along as if I was the other company. What she said really scared me.

"Don't you know what's going on?" she asked. "The detective called and told me that someone is stealing your name. He is a scam artist, his locksmiths are unlicensed, and they may even keep a key to your home!"

The cop had also told her that she should change her locks, for her "safety."

I never disclosed to her that she was not speaking to the other company, but I did assure her that it was just two companies fighting over similar names, and there was no evidence of anyone getting burglarized after the other company did the work.

Can you imagine if you received a call like this? You would be scared also. Even more alarming was when my lawyer learned in disclosure that the detective had also gone through my checking account, called approximately 150 customers, and told them the very same thing. He had kept meticulous records of these phone calls; even writing down each customer's response next to their name.

Interestingly, of the approximately 150 calls this detective made, almost half responded they *Did Not Care* about who changed their locks, so long as the job was done properly (which it was). Some, I will admit, were upset, but only because of the way it was presented to them by the detective. Wouldn't you be upset if a cop called to notify you that a "scam artist" may have a set of keys to your home?

In the end, the only people who really cared were the few customers who thought they had been overcharged by us (after the other companies told them that "we stole business from them" and they "of course" would have done it for less!)

The truth is, locksmithing is a very competitive business, and people will always tell you that they would have done it for less. But the real issue is, who should decide if a customer was overcharged? Is it the responsibility or the right of the state of Florida (or its police officers) to decide on the price they think is fair? Reasonable minds can differ on that point, but it is irrelevant here as, again, the state declined to pass the law that would have regulated the industry.

So, what did the town of Palm County accomplish after an

Conclusion

eight-month investigation that included forensic experts and cost a ton of money? Aside from causing a great deal of emotional distress and expense to me, Josh and Peter, the answer is: not much!

Peter had neither the money nor the stomach to risk a trial, so he agreed to a PTI, which stands for a "Pre-Trial Intervention" (and is also known as "Pre-Trial Diversion"). As described in the chapter on probation, a PTI allows certain first-time offenders to avoid conviction and incarceration. Instead, they agree to be supervised for six or twelve months, after which all charges are completely dismissed (assuming they do not get into any trouble during that time).

Shortly thereafter, Peter ran out of money and had to fire his lawyer. He used a Legal Aid attorney to negotiate the plea, who, in my opinion, did an exceptional job for him. His case wrapped up in less than a year, which is swift compared to most criminal cases. What really pleased me was that the state of Florida had to pay for it.

Why would anyone risk a trial with an offer like this? And since he did stay out of trouble, all charges against Peter were completely dismissed on Nov 20, 2014. In the coming months, under Florida §943, he will be able to have the entire record sealed or expunged (completely destroyed). Although it's a nominal fee, I personally would not waste the money in this case, because since the charges were dismissed, he cannot be denied a professional license in any state.

153

As for Josh, he hired one of the best criminal attorneys in Florida, who did an excellent job as well, to the tune of over $25,000 in legal fees.

In my opinion, he probably did not need to spend so much, as there wasn't a chance in hell that a jury was going to convict him, or Peter, for burglary.

I don't always have faith in the impartiality of juries; however, I truly believe that once they heard how the state of Florida had handled this matter, they would have returned not guilty verdicts for both men.

Remember, the state's entire burglary case was based on Josh entering that woman's house and saying he was from xyz Locksmith. Well, he (and Peter) worked for several locksmiths and would have said yes to any name! It's not like Josh showed up at the customer's house pretending to be a plumber! Chances are the jury would have read between the lines and realized that this was a case of competitors fighting over a trade name, not a criminal act.

Sometimes, I wish these cases had gone to trial and a not guilty verdict handed down by a jury. Then Josh and Peter could have filed suit for wrongful prosecution against Florida. I can't blame anyone for not wanting to risk a trial, though, considering how many innocent people get convicted and how many very guilty people get off scot-free.

Josh's outcome was also favorable—all charges were filed as "nolle prosequi", which is similar to a dismissal. The state could re-file within a short time period in the unlikely event that they uncovered some new evidence against him. Josh's case did take a bit longer to wrap up than Peter's—it began on February 5, 2013 and ended on February 4, 2014—probably so his expensive attorney could earn his fee and do better than Legal Aid. In all likelihood, he spoke with the prosecutor (who happened to be the same person who prosecuted Peter and told him that rather than making Josh take the (PTI) deal, they should just postpone the case for twelve months. If during that time, Josh didn't get in any more trouble, it would be filed as "nolle prosequi". It was a win-win for them—the defense attorney looked good, and the prosecutor didn't have to waste his time, and more taxpayer money, on a trial he would most likely lose.

On October 22, 2014, attorney Jeffrey Weiner, on behalf of Josh, filed a motion to have the record completely expunged. The motion was granted, and the entire record of Josh's arrest was erased from the police files, court records, and Internet searches. As a result, if he is ever asked by a cop or employer, he can lawfully deny or fail to acknowledge being arrested for any crime in connection to this case.

So as you can see, the state of Florida never really had a case. However, they did accomplish part of their mission: they cost us money and taught us a lesson we would never forget.

The last case to be resolved was mine—the so-called "criminal mastermind." I remember reading that in the news and thinking, *mastermind of what?* Sure, maybe our website had gotten us a little extra business; it might not have been nice, but it surely wasn't some criminal enterprise. Every time a bestselling product comes on the market, someone changes it slightly, re-labels it and puts it on the market, and no one ever gets arrested. Under certain circumstances, it is called trademark infringement.

If someone comes out with a similar product or service, the owner of the trademark can take him to civil court, where a judge or jury will decide if the person has truly copied his product. If it is found in the plaintiff's favor, the court may issue an injunction, slap the infringer with a fine and/or a cease-and-desist order, but, again, no one will go to jail over it.

Bottom line, my associates and I angered someone who happened to have a friend in the Palm Beach Police Department. It's that easy to find yourself wrongly charged with some very serious crimes.

Fortunately, my case was assigned a decent prosecutor, who I'll refer to as Bill. On February 14, 2014, Bill and I met to talk about my case. He reviewed all the information from the previous five months and offered me a plea deal. Remember that the state had spent a ton of money on this case, so there was a lot of pressure on him to not dismiss. I didn't blame Bill in any way; he was an extremely decent guy, and like everyone else in the world, he had people to answer to.

I was offered six counts of petty theft—misdemeanors with a total of three years probation. In addition, he was willing to *withhold adjudication* on all counts, which meant that after completing the probation successfully, I would have no criminal conviction.

This was a no-brainer for me. Petty theft is a minor crime, and although I still felt like I had been wronged, it simply wasn't worth it to spend any more money on this case. I was also terrified of the outcome of a trial.

I had done a lot of research on the original charge of "organized scheme to defraud" and read several opinions. Basically, to obtain a conviction, the state only had to prove that my company "misrepresented" itself—*not* that any customers lost any money. It was also irrelevant whether customers were satisfied with our product or service. I knew there was a chance that a jury—which would probably have at least one or two business owners on it—would think I was wrong and deserved a punishment.

It's important to note that the jury was not aware of the sentencing structure and how much jail time I was facing. Sadly, under Florida law, if I were convicted on that count, then I would have automatically been convicted on count two—money laundering.

As I discussed in an earlier chapter, money laundering in the state of Florida is very different from the federal law; all they would have had to do was show that I'd made money while committing an illegal act. At that time, I felt it was not worth risking my freedom to prove a point.

To this day, part of me regrets that I did not have the money or the courage to hire a large law firm, fight the charges, and get a not guilty verdict. If I had won at trial, the state would really have been taught a lesson. But when I thought about it, I realized that the state didn't care. As with every case, they'd use taxpayer money to prosecute me, and if they lost at trial, it would be no big deal to them. For me, however, a win would have made my ego big and my pocketbook small; it also quite possibly could have landed me in prison. That is my whole premise of this book—win or lose, the defendant is *always* the loser!

Every day, ordinary people like you go through this ordeal, and many of them have stories much worse than mine, such as those who were not just wrongly charged with a crime, but *wrongly convicted*. This happens all the time; juries are made up of people, complete with human frailties and errors in judgment. That's why so many people take a plea; either they cannot afford a good attorney to help them in their defense, or the prosecution has convinced them that they will lose at trial.

Despite all the research I did for this book, I was still shocked by the response I received from people who had been wrongly charged and spent money and time fighting the charges, sometimes only to be wrongly convicted anyway. Like me, they had been abused by a legal system supposedly dedicated to safeguarding liberty.

I believe that until the laws of this country are changed to level the playing field for defendants, there will always be innocent people sitting in jail or even executed; others will lose their jobs, their friends and their reputations due to false allegations. That's why ordinary citizens must educate themselves about their rights and remain diligent in fighting for them.

Author's Note

Even as I bring this book to a close, I am still in disbelief over how the actions of one overzealous police officer dramatically changed the lives of three innocent people, personally and professionally. While the eight-month investigation resulted in zero convictions, it did take an enormous toll on me, Josh and Peter, not only in the financial resources and time it took to defend ourselves, but from the stress of not knowing whether we would end up in jail. Our families also suffered greatly, and I attribute, at least in part, my father's death to the emotional upheaval he experienced during this time.

I will always contend that the time and money spent on this case was a waste of taxpayer money, and that, if anything, this was a trademark issue and could have been resolved with a civil suit. You don't have to take my word on this, but the word of three different criminal attorneys—all of whom advised me that my business practices were not criminal. Yet, despite this, the town of Palm Beach continues to congratulate itself for our arrests.

I truly believe that states should be forced to pay all court costs, including attorney's fees, when they lose a case or dismiss it when they figure out they've made a mistake. They would be more careful about who they charge, and a lot of innocent people would not be rotting in jail due to plea deals or false convictions.

I came through my ordeal inspired to help others who have been wrongly charged with a crime, and writing this book was the first step. People are often treated as though they are "guilty until proven innocent"—not the other way around, as promised by the legal system.

Since beginning this project nine months ago, tens of thousands of people have expressed their interest, not only in my story, but in the nuances of the criminal justice system here in Florida. They have viewed my YouTube video, and emailed and called me with their own tragic stories. It is my sincere hope that this book will help people understand their rights under the law, and if it helps even just one person who has been wrongly charged with a crime, I'll know I've done my job.

To that end, I am creating a fund for those who have been victimized by the criminal justice system, and will donate ten percent of the profits from this book to that fund. In the future, I would also like to open a center to help people who have been wrongly charged.

If you or a loved one have been wrongly charged with a crime, contact me by dialing 1-844-wrongly, or "**wrongly" from any cell phone.

It should also be noted that I am currently working on a new book *Life After a Conviction*, which will go into great detail on how to expunge a crime in every state, which states offer it, and if it is not available, other avenues to restore your reputation after a conviction. Visit our website: http:wronglycharged.com for updates.

GLOSSARY OF TERMS

GLOSSARY OF TERMS

Adjudication withheld: If the accused is a first time or non-violent offender, the judge can order probation without a formal conviction. This means that after probation is complete, the person can honestly state (e.g. on a job application) that they were never convicted of the crime. This also makes it possible for you to seal or expunge your record later on.

Appeal: The process by which a person who has either been convicted of a crime or judged liable in a civil suit can dispute the court's ruling. He/she must wait until the trial court has reached a final judgment (a conviction in a criminal case or a decision regarding civil liability) before filing an appeal. In most cases, to get an appeal, the person must first prove that an error occurred during the trial and that the error affected the outcome of the case. If an appeal is granted, the appellate court will review the record with a lot of deference to the trial court's judgment.

All death penalty cases carry an automatic appeal, even if the person sentenced to death does not want it.

One of the most famous appellate cases is *Miranda v. Arizona*, which resulted in the requirement that law enforcement informs a person being arrested of his or her rights, particularly the right to not self-incriminate and the right to counsel.

Arraignment: A court proceeding where the accused is formally charged with a crime, and he/she is apprised of their constitutional rights, including their 6th Amendment right to counsel. For those who have not already hired an attorney, the arraignment may also be their first opportunity to meet their lawyer (i.e. public defender).

Arthur Hearing: A hearing before a judge to determine whether a person accused of a serious felony can get a pre-trial release. Certain offenses, particularly violent crimes, are usually a No Bond Hold, meaning it is assumed the accused will remain in jail until trial; however, the defense can request an Arthur Hearing. If the defense can show that there is not enough evidence to convict and that the accused is not a danger to others and/or a flight risk, the judge may consent to a pretrial release, often with conditions such as electronic (ankle) monitoring.

Bond: Technically, it is a written agreement by which a person promises to pay a certain sum of money if he/she does not perform certain duties properly. In the case of a criminal defendant, he/she is promising that they will remain in the jurisdiction and show up for their court dates. If they do not, whoever posted the bail bond loses any money or collateral they put up to secure the defendant's release from jail.

Booking: The post-arrest process of photographing and fingerprinting a suspect. During booking, law enforcement will also make note of other identifying characteristics, such as a wound or tattoo.

Burden of Proof: In a court case, it is the responsibility of a particular party to prove a fact. For example, in a criminal case, the burden of proof is on the prosecution to prove that the defendant is guilty beyond a reasonable doubt. In a civil case, the burden of proof is on the plaintiff to prove his/her case by a preponderance of the evidence.

Burglary: Under Florida law, burglary is defined as, "Entering a dwelling or structure with the intent of committing an offense and without permission or legal right to be there." The charges are then categorized into a first, second or third-degree felony based on the circumstances. For example:

- If you burglarize a building that is not someone's home, and no one is there during the crime (such as an office building in the middle of the night), you will probably be charged with third-degree burglary and can be sentenced for up to 5 years in prison.

- However, if you rob a home, occupied building or emergency vehicle, or if you plan on stealing a controlled substance from a building, you'll be charged with second-degree burglary and can be sentenced for up to 15 years.

- You will be charged with first-degree burglary if you are armed, commit an assault or battery during the crime, use a motor vehicle to damage the building, or cause more than $1000 in damage to the building. First-degree burglary carries a sentence of up to 30 years in prison and possibly a fine as well.

Civil Action: A lawsuit that is brought about to enforce or protect private rights.

Due Process of Law: The right to the protection of United States' laws, processes and procedures. Due process includes constitutional rights such as the right to counsel, the right to remain silent, the right to a speedy trial, an impartial jury, and to confront our accusers.

Grand Jury: A group of people who meet (often in secret) to decide whether there is probable cause that a crime has been committed and that the accused person committed that crime. The size of a grand jury varies from state to state—in Florida, a grand jury is comprised of 15-21 people, 12 of whom must vote to indict.

Felony: A crime punishable by at least a year in the state prison. Felonies are divided into different categories depending on the severity of the crime. For example:

- **Capital or Life felonies**—these are crimes punishable by death or life in prison and up to a $15,000 fine.

- **First degree felony**—up to 30 years in prison and up to a $10,000 fine, (such as aggravated assault on a police officer.)

- **Second degree felony**—up to fifteen years in prison and up to a $10,000 fine, (such as selling drugs to a minor.)

- **Third degree felony**—up to five years in prison and up to a $5,000 fine, (such as car theft.)

Please note that Florida has recidivist sentencing (or the "Three Strikes" rule). That means if you have already been convicted of two felonies and are later convicted of a third, you can be a given a lengthier prison sentence.

First or "Initial" Appearance: After his or her arrest, this is when the defendant goes before a judge to determine whether or not there was probable cause for the arrest.

Fraud: A false representation intended to deceive another person.

Harmless Error: An error committed during a trial that was either corrected or was not serious enough to affect the outcome of a trial and therefore was not harmful enough to be reversed on appeal.

Indigent: Poor or needy. An indigent defendant may be assigned a court-appointed attorney at no charge to him or her.

Malicious Prosecution: When a prosecutor brings a case against someone without probable cause and with the intent to hurt that person.

Misdemeanor: A crime, less severe than a felony, that is punishable by up to one year in the county jail. A misdemeanor conviction may also carry a fine—up to $1000 for a first-degree misdemeanor and up to $500 for a second-degree misdemeanor. An example of a first-degree misdemeanor is theft of property worth more than $100 and less than $300, while prostitution is a second-degree misdemeanor.

Money Laundering: In Florida, money laundering is defined as transactions designed to hide money obtained through criminal activities. The prosecutor must prove that the person knew the transaction was being done for the purpose of hiding such money. The transactions can range from the exchange of currency and investments to handing over the title to a car or house. Money laundering is a felony and, like other crimes, depends upon the value of the transactions.

- Transactions occurring over a twelve-month period and totaling between $300 and $20,000 is a third-degree felony, punishable by up to 5 years in prison.

- Transactions occurring over a twelve-month period and totaling between $20,000 and $100,000 is a second degree felony, punishable by up to 15 years.

- Transactions occurring over a twelve-month period and exceeding $100,000 is a first-degree felony, punishable by up to 30 years.

Those convicted of money laundering may also have to pay a fine to the state. The amount of the fine can be $250,000 or double the total amount of transactions, whichever is greater. Prior convictions for money laundering can increase the fine to $500,000 or five times the total amount of the financial transactions.

Nebbia Hold: This is when an accused person seeking a bail bond must first prove that the money he/she is putting up for bail did not come from criminal activity (such as drug dealing or money laundering).

Nolo Contendere: This is a plea of "no contest" by a defendant, in which he/she is neither admitting nor denying the charges but is accepting a plea agreement.

Nolle Prosequi: A dismissal of charges before trial. The prosecutor is essentially declining to proceed to trial.

Obtaining Property by False Impersonation: This is a crime by which a person impersonates someone else in order to take property. It's considered larceny and can be charged as a misdemeanor or felony depending on the value of the property taken.

Organized Scheme to Defraud: This crime falls under the Florida Communication Fraud Act, which updated Florida's existing fraud laws to include fraudulent transactions over the Internet, telephone, wire, and other forms of technology. In order to prove this crime, the state must show:

An ongoing or continuous series of acts with an intent to defraud by obtaining value through false promises or representations, or intentionally misrepresenting a future act.

Each act of communication can be charged separately, or the prosecutor can seek to prove many "continuous acts" (e.g., emails sent over the life of a business).

The penalties for this crime are very harsh and depend

on the amount of value defrauded. If less than $20,000 was taken, it is a third-degree felony punishable by up to 5 years in state prison; if $20,000 or more (but less than $50,000) was taken, it is a second-degree felony punishable by up to 15 years; and if $50,000 or more was taken, it is a first-degree felony and punishable by up to 30 years in the state prison.

Plea Bargain: When the defendant in a criminal case pleads guilty to a lesser crime in exchange for reduced or no time jail time. Many people plead guilty to crimes they did not commit because they fear going to trial.

Preliminary Hearing: Similar to a grand jury hearing, except a *judge* determines whether there is sufficient evidence to bring the defendant to trial. The defendant does not have to be present at his/her preliminary hearing.

Pretrial Diversion: The state will offer certain first-time offenders the opportunity to go into an alternative program. The offender is usually supervised for six to twelve months, and if they comply with the conditions of their release, the state will drop the charges, allowing them to avoid a conviction, jail time and a criminal record.

Probation: A suspension of a sentence. Instead of going to jail (or after getting out of the jail), the defendant remains under the supervision of a probation officer for a specified period of time. During this time, he/she must comply with certain conditions. If he/she violates these conditions (and therefore, probation), he/she can be sent to jail for the maximum sentence allowable for the crime.

Pro se (also called pro per): When a person chooses to represent him or herself in a criminal or civil case instead of engaging an attorney, he or she is pro se.

Release on Recognizance: This is when the charge is so minor that no bail is needed.

Restitution: A court order forcing the defendant to make the victim whole, financially or otherwise, for the damage he/she caused.

Scoresheet: A point system that is used to determine the length of sentences for certain crimes, particularly felonies. Florida uses such a scoresheet.

Seal or Expunge: Under Florida law, a person's criminal record is public. However, in certain situations, an arrest may be "expunged", meaning removed from your criminal record or "sealed", meaning most people cannot gain access it. There are some differences between the two, however, one important similarity is that you can *legally deny* having been arrested for the offense. The guidelines for sealing or expunging are set forth by the Florida Department of Law Enforcement. A critical thing to remember is that you can only seal or expunge if you have not been convicted (either because the state dropped the charge or the court withheld adjudication). In addition, you cannot have been convicted of any other crime.

Speedy Trial: Defendants have the right to a speedy trial. Under the Florida Rules of Criminal Procedure, "speedy" is 90 days for a misdemeanor and 175 days for a felony.

Standard of Proof: This is the standard that must be

met in order to achieve a particular result in court. The standard of proof in a criminal case is very high—*beyond a reasonable doubt*—meaning if the judge or jurors have a reasonable doubt that the person didn't do it, he/she must be set free. In a civil case, the standards of proof are a much lower. A *preponderance of the evidence* is the lighter of the two standards and means a fact is more likely to be true than not. The other standards used in civil matters—*clear and convincing evidence*—is more stringent and means a fact is highly or substantially more probable to be true than not.

Supersedeas Bond: also known as an "appeal bond", this is a type of surety bond that allows a defendant to wait to pay a judgment until after the appeal is over. Essentially, it's good faith money that lets the court know the defendant has the means and the intent should he/she lose the appeal. In Florida, a supersedeas bond is limited to no more than $50 million per appellant. That said, the amount of the bond is often more than the judgment, so it can cover additional costs that result from the appeal.

Trademark Infringement: When a trademark (for example, the Nike "swoosh") is registered, the owner is given exclusive use of that mark. When another person or company uses the same or similar trademark (usually to confuse consumers) they are said to have infringed on that exclusive use. The person who owns the trademark can then sue the infringer in civil court under the Lanham Act. If they win, they can get an injunction (force the infringer to stop using the mark); they may often get damages and court costs from the infringer.

APPENDIX

Case Details:

Full Name	DAVID	**DOB**	
Name Suffix		**Sex**	M
Case #		**Race**	White
Status	Closed	**Fee Balance**	0.00
Citation #		**Division**	X: Felony - X
Booking #		**Speedy Trial Du**	2/12/2014

Court Events

Date	Time	Event Type	Location	Room	Notes
10/10/2013	8:30 AM	STF - STATE TO FILE CHARGES	MB	10F (Main Branch)	
12/20/2013	8:30 AM	CANCELLED - CD - CASE DISPOSITION	MB	10F (Main Branch)	ARRAINGMENT
1/10/2014	8:30 AM	CD - CASE DISPOSITION	MB	10F (Main Branch)	
2/14/2014	8:30 AM	STCK - STATUS CHECK	MB	10F (Main Branch)	DEFT MUST BE PRESENT

Parties

Full Name	Party Type	Sex	Race	Date of Birth	AKA	Deceased	Sheriffs #	Hair	Eyes
DAVID	DEFENDANT	M	White					Black	BROWN

Charges

Count	Statute #	Description	Disposition	Disposition Date	Sentence
1	896.101(35A)	MONEY LAUNDERING	NOLLE PROSSE	2/14/2014	
2	817.034(4A3)	ORGANIZED SCHEME TO DEFRAUD	NOLLE PROSSE	2/14/2014	
3	812.014(12E)	PETIT THEFT (VALUE OF $100.00 OR MORE)	ADJUDICATION WITHHELD	2/14/2014	
4	812.014(12E)	PETIT THEFT (VALUE OF $100.00 OR MORE)	ADJUDICATION WITHHELD	2/14/2014	
5	812.014(12E)	PETIT THEFT (VALUE OF $100.00 OR MORE)	ADJUDICATION WITHHELD	2/14/2014	
6	812.014(12E)	PETIT THEFT (VALUE OF $100.00 OR MORE)	ADJUDICATION WITHHELD	2/14/2014	
7	812.014(12E)	PETIT THEFT (VALUE OF $100.00 OR MORE)	ADJUDICATION WITHHELD	2/14/2014	
8	812.014(12E)	PETIT THEFT (VALUE OF $100.00 OR MORE)	ADJUDICATION WITHHELD	2/14/2014	
9	817.02	OBTAIN PROPERTY BY FALSE PERSONATION	NO ACTION TAKEN BY PROSECUTOR	10/9/2013	

Main Parties

Judge:

State Attorney:

Defense Attorney:

Co-Counsel:

Linked Cases
No Linked Cases Found.

Warrants/Service Docs

Warrant/Document Type	Warrant #/Document ID	Issue Date	Last Action Date	Status/Return Reason	Last Action
DIRECT FILE CAPIAS/ WARRANT		8/16/2013	8/22/2013	Executed	Returned

Wrongly Charged

Case Details:

Full Name	JOSH	**DOB**	
Name Suffix		**Sex**	M
Case #		**Race**	W
Status	Closed	**Fee Balance**	0.00
Citation #		**Division**	S: Felony - S
Booking #		**Speedy Trial Du**	7/30/2013

Court Events

Date	Time	Event Type	Location	Room	Notes
2/6/2013	9:00 AM	FAP - FIRST APPEARANCE	GB	#1 (Gun Club)	
3/7/2013	10:30 AM	CANCELLED - FAP - FIRST APPEARANCE	GB	#1 (Gun Club)	BONDED
3/28/2013	8:30 AM	STF - STATE TO FILE CHARGES	MB	11E (Main Branch)	
5/13/2013	8:30 AM	CANCELLED - CD - CASE DISPOSITION	MB	11E (Main Branch)	
5/13/2013	2:45 PM	CD - CASE DISPOSITION	MB	11E (Main Branch)	
7/8/2013	9:30 AM	CANCELLED - CD - CASE DISPOSITION	MB	11F (Main Branch)	
7/15/2013	11:00 AM	CD - CASE DISPOSITION	MB	11E (Main Branch)	
1/27/2014	11:00 AM	CANCELLED - STCK - STATUS CHECK	MB	11E (Main Branch)	
2/13/2014	8:30 AM	STCK - STATUS CHECK	MB	11E (Main Branch)	
10/22/2014	8:30 AM	MH - MOTION HEARING	MB	11H (Main Branch)	RE: TO EXPUNGE

Main Parties

Judge:

State Attorney:

Defense Attorney:

Co-Counsel:

Parties

Full Name	Party Type	Sex	Race	Date of Birth	AKA	Deceased	Sheriffs #	Hair	Eyes
JOSH	DEFENDANT	M	W						

Charges

Count	Statute #	Description	Disposition	Disposition Date	Sentence
1	810.02(13)	BURGLARY OF A DWELLING	NOLLE PROSSE	2/13/2014	
2	812.014(12D)	GRAND THEFT FROM A DWELLING	NOLLE PROSSE	2/13/2014	
3	817.02	OBTAIN PROPERTY BY FALSE PERSONATION	NO ACTION TAKEN BY PROSECUTOR	3/28/2013	

Linked Cases
No Linked Cases Found.

Sentences
No Sentences Found.

Warrants/Service Docs
No Warrants/Service Docs Found.

Arrests

Arresting Agency	Agency Number	Booking #	Incident #	Arrest/Offense Date
Town of Palm Beach PD				2/5/2013

Appendix

Bonds

Bond #	Type	Count	Bondsman	Depositor	Surety Company	Closed Date	Amount
	None	1				2/6/2013	$0.00
	Per Schedule	2				2/6/2013	$3,000.00
	Per Schedule	3				2/6/2013	$3,000.00
	Court Ordered	1				2/8/2013	$5,000.00
	Court Ordered	2				2/8/2013	$3,000.00
	Court Ordered	3				2/6/2013	$3,000.00
X110020096	Surety	1	BARBIES BAIL BONDS			2/13/2014	$5,000.00
X110020094	Surety	2	BARBIES BAIL BONDS		U.S. SPECIALTY INSURANCE COMPANY	2/13/2014	$3,000.00
X110020095	Surety	3	BARBIES BAIL BONDS		U.S. SPECIALTY INSURANCE COMPANY	3/28/2013	$3,000.00

Total Fees

Total Amount Due: $47.00   Total Amount Paid: $47.00   Total Balance: $0.00   Total Judgment Interest: $0.00
Total Balance + Interest: $0.00

Fees

Effective Date	Due Date	Description	Amount Due	Amount Paid	Balance	In Collections	In Judgment
2/6/2013	2/6/2013	Indigent PD Application Fee PB	$0.00	$0.00	$0.00		
7/30/2014	7/30/2014	Criminal Seal or Expunge Fee PB	$42.00	$42.00	$0.00		
10/22/2014	10/22/2014	Criminal Service Fees PB	$5.00	$5.00	$0.00		

Payment Plans

No Payment Plans Found.

Wrongly Charged

Case Details:

Full Name	PETER	DOB	
Name Suffix		Sex	M
Case #		Race	W
Status	Closed	Fee Balance	0.00
Citation #		Division	W: Felony - W
Booking #		Speedy Trial Du	8/2/2013

Court Events

Date	Time	Event Type	Location	Room	Notes
2/9/2013	9:00 AM	FAP - FIRST APPEARANCE	GB	#1 (Gun Club)	
3/11/2013	10:30 AM	CANCELLED - FAP - FIRST APPEARANCE	GB	#1 (Gun Club)	
4/4/2013	8:30 AM	STF - STATE TO FILE CHARGES	MB	11F (Main Branch)	
5/14/2013	8:30 AM	CD - CASE DISPOSITION	MB	11F (Main Branch)	
7/15/2013	8:30 AM	STCK - STATUS CHECK	MB	11F (Main Branch)	COMP OF DISC
7/15/2013	8:30 AM	CANCELLED - STCK - STATUS CHECK	MB	11E (Main Branch)	COMP OF DISC
9/4/2013	8:30 AM	STCK - STATUS CHECK	MB	11F (Main Branch)	
9/27/2013	8:30 AM	CANCELLED - STCK - STATUS CHECK	MB	11F (Main Branch)	
10/2/2013	8:30 AM	PC - PLEA CONFERENCE	MB	11F (Main Branch)	

Parties

Full Name	Party Type	Sex	Race	Date of Birth	AKA	Deceased	Sheriffs #	Hair	Eyes
PETER	DEFENDANT	M	W					Brown	Blue

Charges

Count	Statute #	Description	Disposition	Disposition Date	Sentence	Offense Date	Sentence Status
1	810.02(1)(4)	BURGLARY OF A STRUCTURE OR CONVEYANCE	NOLLE PROSSE	10/2/2013		12/14/2012	
2	812.014(12D)	GRAND THEFT FROM A DWELLING	NOLLE PROSSE	10/2/2013		12/17/2012	

Main Parties

Judge: Defense Attorney:

State Attorney:

Linked Cases
No Linked Cases Found.

Sentences
No Sentences Found.

Arrests

Arresting Agency	Agency Number	Booking #	Incident #	Arrest/Offense Date
Town of Palm Beach PD	76			2/8/2013

Warrants/Service Docs
No Warrants/Service Docs Found.

Bonds

Bond #	Type	Count	Bondsman	Depositor	Surety Company

Appendix

IN THE DISTRICT COURT OF APPEAL OF THE STATE OF FLORIDA
FOURTH DISTRICT   JULY TERM 1989

DAVID MERKATZ,   )   NOT FINAL UNTIL TIME EXPIRES
)   TO FILE REHEARING MOTION
            Appellant,   )   AND, IF FILED, DISPOSED OF.
)
v.   )   CASE NO. 89-0178.
)
DEPARTMENT OF STATE,   )
DIVISION OF LICENSING,   )
)
            Appellee.   )
_____)

Opinion filed   December 20, 1989

Appeal from the State of Florida,
Department of State, Division of
Licensing.

Cynthia A. Greenfield of Cynthia ·
A. Greenfield, P.A., Miami, for
appellant.

Mimi Daigle, Assistant General
Counsel, Department of State,
Tallahassee, for appellee.

PER CURIAM.

        We reverse and remand with directions that appellant's

application be granted since it is undisputed that appellant's

civil rights were restored in New York and that the offense for

which he was convicted would not constitute a felony or cause the

loss of his civil rights in Florida. See § 790.23(2), Fla. Stat.

(1987).

ANSTEAD, GLICKSTEIN and WARNER, JJ., concur.

M A N D A T E

from

DISTRICT COURT OF APPEAL OF THE STATE OF FLORIDA

FOURTH DISTRICT

This cause having been brought to this Court by appeal, and after due consideration the Court having issued its opinion; YOU ARE HEREBY COMMANDED that such further proceedings be had in said cause as may be in accordance with the opinion of this Court, and with the rules of procedure and laws of the State of Florida.

WITNESS the Honorable George W. Hersey, Chief Judge of the District Court of Appeal of the State of Florida, Fourth District, and seal of the said Court at West Palm Beach, Florida on this day.

DATE:____January 5, 1990_____   **A TRUE**

CASE NO.:____89-0178_____   **COPY**

COUNTY OF ORIGIN:__Dept. of State, Division of Licensing____

T.C. CASE NO.:__WPB 88-21_____

STYLE:__Merkatz v. Dept. of State_____

Clyde L. Heath, Clerk
District Court of Appeal
Fourth District

ORIGINAL TO: Dept. of State, Division of Licensing

CC: Cynthia A. Greenfield, Esq.
     Mimi Daigle, Assistant General Counsel

/djm

178

STATE OF NEW YORK

CERTIFICATE OF RELIEF FROM DISABILITIES

FOR COURT OR BOARD OF PAROLE
Docket, File, or other Identifying No.

This certificate is issued to the holder to grant relief from all or certain enumerated disabilities, forfeitures, or bars to his employment automatically imposed by law by reason of his conviction of the crime or of the offense specified herein.
This certificate shall NOT be deemed nor construed to be a pardon.
SEE REVERSE SIDE FOR EXPLANATION OF THE LAW GOVERNING THIS CERTIFICATE
The Original Certificate is to be presented to the person to whom awarded. One copy is to be retained by the issuing agency, and one copy is to be filed with the N.Y.S. Div. of Criminal Justice Services, Executive Park, Stuyvesant Plaza, Albany, N.Y. 12203

1. For use by DCJS	HOLDER OF CERTIFICATE			3. NYSID Number (if not known, supply fingerprints to DCJS. If fingerprints are unobtainable, complete items 15-18 below.)
	2. Last Name	First Name	Middle Initial	
	Merkatz	David		

4. Crime or offense for which convicted	5. Date of arrest	6. Date of sentence
Criminal Mischief III		

7. Court of disposition (Court, Part, Term, Venue)	8. Certificate issued by:
Part B, Kings Supreme Court Judge Golden	a [ ] COURT INDICATED IN NO. 7 b [ ] STATE BOARD OF PAROLE

9. Date this certificate issued	10. If this Certificate replaces Certificate of Relief From Disabilities previously issued, give date of previous Certificate.
10/12/83	Date: _____ [X] Not Applicable

11. CHECK ONE BOX ONLY

This certificate shall:

a [ ] Relieve the holder of all forfeitures, and of all disabilities and bars to employment, excluding the right to retain or to be eligible for public office, by virtue of the fact that this certificate is issued at the time of sentence. The Date of Sentence in this case must agree with the Date Certificate Issued.

b [X] Relieve the holder of all disabilities and bars to employment, excluding the right to be eligible for public office.

c [ ] Relieve the holder of the forfeitures, disabilities or bars hereinafter enumerated _____

12. [X] This certificate shall be considered permanent.

[ ] This certificate shall be considered temporary until _____. After this date, unless revoked earlier by the issuing court or parole board, this certificate shall be considered permanent. A person who knowingly uses or attempts to use a revoked certificate in order to obtain or exercise any right or privilege that he would not be entitled to obtain or to exercise without valid certificate shall be guilty of a misdemeanor.

13. Signature of issuing official(s)	Print or type name(s)	14. Title(s)
(signature)	ELLIOT GOLDEN	SUPREME COURT JUSTICE

Complete the following for DCJS, only if fingerprints are not obtainable

15. Sex	16. Color	17. Height	18. Date of Birth (Month, Day, Year)

LAWS GOVERNING THE ISSUANCE OF CERTIFICATES OF RELIEF FROM DISABILITIES

(The laws governing the issuance of certificates of relief from disabilities are set forth in Article 23 of the New York State Correction Law. The excerpts below summarize certain portions of those laws and are set forth merely for convenience. They are not intended as administrative interpretations and they do not relieve any party of full knowledge of and compliance with the applicable provisions of law.)

This certificate is issued to relieve the holder, an "eligible offender" as defined in § 700 of the Correction Law, of all or of enumerated forfeitures, disabilities, or bars to employment automatically imposed by law by reason of his conviction of the crime or offense specified on the face of this certificate.

This certificate shall be considered a "temporary certificate" where (1) issued by a court to a holder who is under a "revocable sentence" as defined in § 700 of the Correction Law and the court's authority to revoke such sentence has not expired, or (2) issued by the State Board of Parole and the holder is still under the supervision of the Board. Where the holder is under a revocable sentence, this certificate may be revoked by the court for violation of the conditions of such sentence and shall be revoked by the court if it revokes the sentence and commits the holder to an institution under the jurisdiction of the State Department of Correctional Services. Where the holder is subject to the supervision of the State Board of Parole, this certificate may be revoked by the Board for violation of the conditions of parole or release. Any such revocation shall be upon notice and after an opportunity to be heard. If this certificate is not so revoked, it shall become a permanent certificate upon expiration or termination of the court's authority to revoke the sentence or upon termination of the jurisdiction of the Board of Parole over the holder.

RIGHTS OF RELIEF FROM DISABILITIES

A. Where the certificate is issued by a court at the time sentence is pronounced, it covers forfeitures as well as disabilities. In any other case the certificate applies only to disabilities.

B. A conviction of the crime or the offense specified on the face of this certificate shall NOT cause automatic forfeiture of any license, permit, employment or franchise, including the right to register for or vote at an election, or automatic forfeiture of any other right or privilege, held by the eligible offender and covered by the certificate. Nor shall such conviction be deemed to be a conviction within the meaning of any provision of law that imposes, by reason of a conviction, a bar to any employment, a disability to exercise any right or a disability to apply for or to receive any license, permit or other authority or privilege, covered by the certificate. Provided, however, that no such certificate shall apply, or be construed so as to apply, to the right of such person to retain or to be eligible for public office.

C. A conviction of the crime or the offense specified on the face of this certificate shall NOT prevent any judicial, administrative, licensing or other body, board or authority from relying upon the conviction specified on the reverse side of this certificate as the basis for the exercise of its discretionary power to suspend, revoke, refuse to issue or renew any license, permit or other authority or privilege.

180

INDEX

R

Right against self-incrimination 39

W

www.ingramcontent.com/pod-product-compliance
Lightning Source LLC
Chambersburg PA
CBHW072138270326
41931CB00010B/1802